The NATIONAL BOARD CERTIFICATION *Handbook*

SUPPORT & STORIES *from* TEACHERS & CANDIDATES

Edited by Diane Barone
University of Nevada, Reno

Foreword by Beverly Ann Chin

Stenhouse Publishers
Portland, Maine

Stenhouse Publishers
www.stenhouse.com

Library of Congress Cataloging-in-Publication Data
The National Board certification handbook : support and stories from teachers and candidates / edited by Diane Barone.
    p.   cm.
    Includes bibliographical references (p.).
    ISBN 1-57110-349-X (alk. paper)
    1. National Board for Professional Teaching Standards (U.S.—Handbooks, manuals, etc. 2. Teachers—Certification—Standards—United States—Handbooks, manuals, etc. 3. Teaching—Standards—United States—Handbooks, manuals, etc. I. Barone, Diane M.
LB 1771.N393 2002
371.12—dc21   2002017595

Cover photo of Jeannine Paszek

Manufactured in the United States of America on acid-free paper
06 05 04 03 02 9 8 7 6 5 4 3 2 1

*This book is dedicated to
accomplished teachers and their students.*

Contents

Foreword

National Board Certification is one of the most profound professional development initiatives of our teaching profession. It reflects accomplished teaching practice based on high and rigorous standards. To receive National Board Certification, teachers document their classroom practice through an extensive process of performance-based assessments and written exercises. As teachers select, describe, analyze, and reflect on their teaching practices, they provide evidence of how they meet the standards of the National Board for Professional Teaching Standards (NBPTS). National Board Certified Teachers are educators who have demonstrated accomplished teaching in their subject area with their students.

The NBPTS is dedicated to identifying, recognizing, and celebrating accomplished teaching in America. We want to encourage and sustain the professional growth of teachers and to promote the best education for all students. Through its standards and assessments, the National Board for Professional Teaching Standards is transforming the teaching profession at all stages of our careers—from beginning teachers to experienced teachers—and at all levels of the educational system—from kindergarten through graduate school.

In 1995, the NBPTS named its first eighty-six National Board Certified Teachers. As of January 2002, there are 16,035 National Board Certified Teachers in fifty states and the District of Columbia. Each year, the number of candidates grows. Our goal is to have 100,000 National Board Certified Teachers by 2006, so that every school in America will benefit from the expertise of a National Board Certified Teacher.

National Board Certification is the highest recognition of accomplished teaching. As candidates read the NBPTS standards and reflect on their teaching of students and subject matter, teachers strengthen their classroom practice, which, in turn, benefits the students and improves their learning. As candidates discuss with each other the samples of their students' work and the videotapes of their teaching, they become mentors, coaches, and critical friends who encourage each other to grow as professionals. Teachers who immerse themselves in the certification process are truly engaged in an extensive, yearlong professional development that is meaningful and relevant for both teachers and students.

As a mentor for candidates for National Board Certification, I meet National Board Certified Teachers and candidates all across the nation. Candidates often have questions as they think about pursuing certification: Am I prepared to undertake the intensive yearlong process? Do I have the knowledge, skills, and disposition to achieve National Board Certification? Will my particular teaching context and school curriculum be accommodated in the certificate standards? Will my individual style and creativity be acknowledged in my portfolio? Will my students benefit from my certification? Will the rewards be worth all the time and energy?

The National Board Certification Handbook: Stories and Strategies from Teachers and Candidates addresses all these questions and more with straightforward advice and personal experiences from one group of candidates. Through each teacher's story, we gain a clear understanding of the certification process and a deep appreciation of the many ways teachers demonstrate integration of the standards into their own classrooms with their own students. The teachers describe their thoughts and feelings as they learned about National Board Certification, decided to become candidates, developed and submitted their portfolios, prepared for the assessment center exercises, and awaited their results. Each teacher offers useful suggestions, checklists, and resources to help other candidates engaged in this complex and challenging certification process. We celebrate their journeys of professional development and empowerment. Their individual and collective voices inspire all teachers to embrace the vision of the National Board for Professional Teaching Standards.

The National Board Certification Handbook is a valuable resource for candidates, their mentors, and other individuals who wish to understand how the process of National Board Certification transforms teachers' professional lives and strengthens students' learning. As you read this book, I invite you to reflect on your own growth as a professional educator and to celebrate the process of National Board Certification.

Beverly Ann Chin, *NBPTS Board Member (1995–2003)*
University of Montana, Missoula, MT

Acknowledgments

The genesis of this book was a conversation among teacher candidates for certification by the National Board for Professional Teaching Standards. They had just completed the portfolio part of the process and were preparing for the assessment center exercises. We took a detour from this preparation and talked about all that we had learned through this process. We decided that other teachers would benefit from our experiences and thought that the best vehicle for this support would be a book. We left that meeting thinking about what would be most important to share with other candidates.

I would like to thank these teachers for the straightforward suggestions that they offered to others. The teachers who contributed directly to this book are Mandy Campbell, Cora Carrigan, Jessica Daniels, Carol Hines, Leo McBride, Petrina McCarty-Puhl, Jeannine Paszek, Barbara Surritte, Margaret Thiel, and Jeanine VanDeVort. These teachers' words are shared in the book, but the entire cohort of teachers influenced what we wrote. The other teachers in this cohort were Ginny Beck, Kindra Cerfoglio, Yvette Deighton, Stacy Drum, Mark Hurst, Kathy King, Franz Nenzel, Kathy Redding, and Sue Vaughn.

Beyond this group of very accomplished teachers, I would like to thank my dean, William Sparkman, for his generosity in starting the National Board project at my university. He understood how important this project is to recognizing accomplished teaching in our community. I need to thank Skip Wenda of the Nevada State Department of Education.

He found the financial support to help teachers engage in this process and helped the state legislature understand the importance of rewarding teachers after they became certified.

Finally, we thank Philippa Stratton and William Varner for their encouragement and quality of editing this book at Stenhouse. We know it is better because of them.

Contributors

Diane Barone is a professor of Literacy Studies at the University of Nevada, Reno, where she teaches courses in early literacy, diversity, and qualitative research. She also facilitates groups of teachers seeking National Board Certification. Additionally, she is the editor of *Reading Research Quarterly.*

Mandy Campbell is now in her eleventh year of teaching high school English. After spending three years in the U.S. Army as a medic, Mandy earned her Bachelor of Science degree in Secondary Education majoring in both English and Health. In 1993, she earned her Master of Arts in the teaching of English from the University of Nevada, Reno. She loves teaching and attending her students' games and events, and is proud to be her school's scholarship director and advisor to the National Honor Society.

Carol T. Hines spends the school year teaching seventh-grade social studies at Darrel C. Swope Middle School in Reno, Nevada. She is active in school programs and is a member of the district's Cadre of Teacher Trainers. She holds both elementary and secondary teaching credentials and achieved the level of National Board Certified Teacher, Early Adolescent/Generalist in 2000. As an educational consultant, she presents at conferences and conducts staff development workshops at the national, state, and local levels on implementing hands-on, active-learning curriculum materials.

Leo McBride has taught English and is currently the drama instructor and Fine Arts department leader at McQueen High School in Reno, Nevada. He is entering his eleventh year of teaching. He has a master's degree in Theater Directing from Roosevelt University in Chicago. He has been married to his high school sweetheart, Nancy, for twenty-five years and they have one dog, Chi Chi.

Introduction

*I want to become a National Board teacher so what do I have to do?
I have no idea where to begin. Can you send me some information
about it? Do I just take a test? If so, where and when can I do it? I am
confused but I want to do this. Can you help?*

Since 1999, when I began to work with teachers who wanted to achieve National Board Certification, I have often heard these questions and concerns. Before we began our collaboration, I had been sent by the dean of the college where I teach to find out about this process.

When I returned, I sent out my first recruitment flyer to teachers. Shortly after, I met with about forty teachers who expressed interest. From this group, nineteen teachers chose to engage in the process and work with me as their facilitator. These were brave teachers, very brave. They taught in elementary schools and high schools in rich and poor neighborhoods. The group was split between high school and elementary school teachers with only one middle school teacher. Most of the teachers taught in regular classes but one teacher was an elementary special education teacher and another taught only children for whom English was a new language. Although their placements varied, the teachers were similar in the passion they brought to teaching and the high expectations they held for their students. They celebrated their students who were successful academically and they worried about how to help others experience success. They scrutinized their teaching practices and revised them moment by moment if that was required. They considered themselves professional educators and cared very much about their practice.

In addition, this was the first group of teachers in the state of Nevada to seek this certification. At the time we started to work together, we lived in the only state that had no National Board Certified Teachers (NBCTs). So we entered the process with minimal knowledge of its details, but with a passion to share the exemplary teaching and learning that were happening in our community. We spent one year learning about the intricacies of documenting this teaching and learning for the National Board. This learning did not always happen easily. We went to many sources as we tried to figure out the expectations for successful completion of this process.

At the end of the year we had a new passion, and that was to share what we had learned. We wanted teachers to know that the process is complex and rigorous, but that there are strategic ways to engage in it. We wanted teachers to know that there are no simple answers to their questions about the process, but that there is information to help with their decisions about it and support for them as they pursue this certification.

Throughout this book, the teachers and I share the power of this certification process and how it changed us forever. Individually and collectively, we will never look at teaching and learning as we did before we started. Never again will we underestimate the power of an accomplished teacher to make a difference in the lives of students. We all learned what Jenni Day (2001) conveys so eloquently:

> Exemplary teaching ability is not a magical, mystical thing that people either have or don't have. It develops as teachers become expert observers of students and learning, as they seek continually to learn and grow, and as they reflect on their own teaching and experiences in learning. (p. 216)

Teachers' voices are strong in this book. They tell of their journeys through this process, warts and all. They want other candidates to benefit from the lessons they learned along the way. They want teachers to know that achieving this certification does not mean that a teacher must fit some predetermined criteria that lead to a loss of individuality. This is an important message. They do not teach in the same ways and they do not teach the same subjects, but they all teach to the highest standards. To do so, they call on their strength as teachers, their ability to teach to the highest standards, their competence in matching instruction to individual students' needs, their knowledge of content and how to convey it to students, their methods of making parents part of the teaching and learning process, and their willingness to share this with others to improve the learning of all students.

This book is composed of practical chapters with a multitude of suggestions and teachers' chapters with their stories and practical support for candidates engaged in this process. Throughout the book, the teachers offer strategies and materials that helped them through the process.

There is much that teachers need to know about this endeavor before taking on this challenge. The goal of this book is to give you, a teacher considering this certification or engaged with it, the necessary information to make this decision and then to provide support to you once you have begun the process.

The book is organized into six chapters. Chapter 1, "What Is National Board Certification Anyway?" serves as a foundation chapter. In this chapter, Diane Barone gives an overview of the assessment process, the expectations for teachers, and the available certificates. In Chapter 2, "Reflections in a Human Mirror," Carol T. Hines provides suggestions for each aspect of the assessment process. Her chapter is rich with helpful hints. Chapter 3, "Support Through the Whole Process: The Nitty-Gritty Issues" is the longest and perhaps the most practical chapter. This chapter deals with all the issues that you will need to consider as you engage in this process. In Chapter 4, "Freshwater Fish in a Saltwater Pond," Leo McBride shares how hard it can be to find the right certification area. He chose Adolescent and Young Adult English and Language Arts, but he found this area problematic because he is a drama teacher. His story will help other teachers think carefully about choosing the right certificate area for them. In Chapter 5, "And Miles to Go Before I Sleep," Mandy Campbell walks teachers through the whole assessment process. She shares how many hours it takes to complete such a rigorous process. The last chapter, "All Those Questions," lists answers to common questions about the process. This book reveals how complex and individualized the journey to National Board Certification is.

Earning certification as a National Board teacher is a process that requires teachers to enter bravely into risky territory. And although the journey will probably be filled with detours and perhaps frustrations, the result is breathtaking. Now these teachers are recognized by their families, friends, schools, local communities, and local and state governments for their exemplary teaching. Their accomplishments show all stakeholders in education that teachers are professionals, and that it is *teachers* that make the difference in student learning and achievement.

1

What Is National Board Certification Anyway?

Diane Barone

Reading the literature, dialoguing with other colleagues, and engaging in inquiry allows us to sharpen our ability to see what matters in our teaching. This recursive process allows us to hone our listening and observation skills, our ability to analyze learning situations, and the thoughtfulness we apply to writing and reflecting on actions and events and what they seem to mean. This process also helps to ensure that we do not lose sight of what is most important to us—our students. (Dillon 2000, p. 156)

This quote from Deborah Dillon synthesizes the process of becoming a National Board Certified Teacher. The National Board assessment process requires a teacher to reflect on his or her teaching actions, what they mean, and how they result in student learning. This is the heart of this assessment process.

This process is perhaps more important to today's teachers than to teachers in years past. At the beginning of 2001, teachers from preschool to the university were facing criticism from the general public and policy makers. These criticisms typically center on a perceived lack of expertise

on the part of teachers to prepare students of all ages in public school settings (Ray and Laminack 2001). These criticisms are not new to teachers;
they just seem more plentiful in the last few years. One result of these
assaults on teachers and their capabilities has been the adoption of man-
dated programs. These programs script the instruction provided to teachers so that all instruction is similar despite the differing needs of students.
These types of programs have become routine in classrooms, especially in
the classrooms of high-poverty schools. Unfortunately, these programs
look to deskill teachers and remove from them the decision-making
process required of teaching.

However, effective teaching is based on the "minute-to-minute, sec-
ond-to-second execution of discipline and instruction, with all the affec-
tive dimensions of both, that determines whether children are learning in
that classroom" (Cunningham 1999, p. 43). Teaching, not programs,
results in effective learning (Gambrell, Morrow, Neuman, and Pressley
1999). Systemic education reform must involve the classroom, one teacher
at a time, because the individual teacher has direct daily impact on the lives
and learning of individual students.

States, districts, and schools have certainly used ways besides programs to enhance teaching and instruction, ways that are focused on
teachers and thus recognize their importance. Most often these entities
look to professional development as a means to exemplary achievement by
students. Among the options for professional development is the opportunity for teachers to seek certification by the National Board for
Professional Teaching Standards (NBPTS). By pursuing this option, a
teacher demonstrates that he or she can teach to the highest standards.
This certification confirms that a teacher is indeed a capable teacher and
more. He or she provides exemplary instruction to the students in his or
her classroom.

All students can reach high standards if they have teachers who can
meet high standards. Fortunately, many teachers see teaching as a profession that requires the level of commitment and lifetime learning found in
medical, legal, and other professions. These teachers believe that they
should be held to high and rigorous standards of knowledge and skill.
Many of them opt to acquire National Board Certification.

In this chapter I focus on the National Board Certification process in
general. To help you understand this process, Figure 1.1 shares some of the
vocabulary that is unique to it. As teachers work through this process, the

Figure 1.1

National Board Vocabulary

Assessment center The assessment center, usually situated in the community, where each candidate goes for one day or a half-day of assessment. The National Board indicates to teachers the location of the nearest center and how to make an assessment appointment.

Banking A candidate who is not successful in achieving National Board Certification can bank his or her scores and retake portions of the assessment. There is a two-year window for retakes. The candidate is credited with the new score(s) whether they are higher or lower than the original scores.

The Box Each candidate receives a box that contains all the assessment materials, except those related to the assessment center. The candidate sends the completed portfolio to the NBPTS in this box.

Documented accomplishments The candidate writes about an event during which he or she worked with parents or the professional community and that influenced student learning. The format for these accomplishments is provided in materials sent to candidates.

Entries Each candidate completes four entries for his or her portfolio. Certificate areas vary a bit in expectations but most teachers complete two videos and responses to student work.

Instructional artifacts Materials used in a lesson such as assignments, worksheets, resources or handouts, and software.

Letters of verification Letters from professionals that verify an accomplishment that a teacher has detailed.

Standards Each certificate area contains standards specific to the area. For example, in music a teacher would need to meet the standards centered on facilitating music learning, among others.

Student release form Permission from each student and his or her parents or legal guardian to participate in this process and allow the students' work to be used.

Written commentary Text written by a teacher in response to directions for a portfolio entry. For example, a teacher writes a commentary to support a video.

---

language associated with it becomes routine, but this is certainly not the case when first engaging with it.

What Is the National Board?

In 1987, the National Board for Professional Teaching Standards was created as a nonpartisan, independent, and nonprofit organization. Its mission is to establish high and rigorous standards for what accomplished teachers should know and be able to do, to develop and operate a national voluntary system to assess and certify teachers who meet these standards, and to advance related education reforms for the purpose of improving student learning in U.S. schools. Recently, the National Board also engaged in research to document the teaching and learning that occurs in the classrooms of National Board Certified Teachers. Much of this research is shared at the National Board's web site at www.nbpts.org.

Teachers are central to all aspects of the National Board's efforts. In addition to informing policy, teachers serve on standards committees, pilot test portfolio exercises, participate in a speakers bureau, and score the exercises submitted by candidates for National Board Certification. In fact, only practicing classroom teachers may serve as assessors for National Board Certification, and there are numerous scoring centers throughout the United States.

As of this writing, 16,035 teachers have achieved their board certification. Of this number, 7,504 achieved this status during the 2000–2001 year. Most of these teachers are certified as Early Childhood and Middle Childhood Generalists. Clearly, as states provide incentives for National Board Certification, more teachers will tackle this rigorous assessment process.

A teacher can choose to participate in this process only after having taught successfully for three full years. In addition, a candidate must have graduated from an accredited institution and hold a valid state teaching license.

What Is National Board Certification?

National Board Certification is a demonstration of teaching practice measured against high standards. A NBPTS certificate attests that a teacher has been assessed as one who is accomplished, makes sound professional judgments about students' learning, and acts effectively on those judgments. This certification process is undertaken on a voluntary basis. The advanced system of National Board Certification complements, but does not replace, state licensing. It is a professional certification increasingly used by states that have tiered licensure systems as an option for advanced licensing requirements.

To achieve this certification, a teacher must accomplish the following tasks:

1. Build a portfolio that is completed in his or her classroom. The entries for this portfolio center around students' work, videotapes of teaching and student learning, other teaching artifacts (e.g., lesson plans), parent communication, and professional accomplishments. In the Next Generation assessments begun in 2001, a teacher completes four portfolio entries.

2. Support the videos and students' work with written commentaries on the goals and purposes of instruction, reflections of what occurred, the effectiveness of the lesson, and the rationale for professional judgment used.

3. Complete the portfolio entries within four months. This requires 200 to 400, sometimes more, hours.

4. Complete assessment center exercises, which are designed around content knowledge. They allow candidates to demonstrate knowledge about the subject matter highlighted in their certificate area. For the Next Generation certificates, a teacher is at the assessment center for one half-day and completes six, thirty-minute prompts that are centered on content knowledge.

The assessment materials arrive in what has become known as *The Box,* which contains all the details for the portfolio. For many teachers engaged in this process, The Box seems almost to become a live person. For instance, I heard teachers say, "I can't face it. I hid it in the closet." or "I hear the box saying, 'Get to work.'" In reality The Box is the red, white, and blue container that brings the information for each certificate area and the container into which candidates place the completed portfolio for its return to the National Board.

Currently, National Board Certification is available in twenty-three areas and is being developed in twenty-five fields. Figure 1.2 shows the areas for which certificates are available. Certificates are being developed in the areas of language arts, health education, and guidance and counseling. With the variety of certificates available, the National Board's standards and assessments apply to approximately 95 percent of teachers in U.S. elementary and secondary schools.

Figure 1.2

Certificate Areas

Art
Early and middle childhood art (ages 3–12)
Early adolescence through young adulthood art (ages 11–18+)

Career and Technical Education
Early adolescence through young adulthood career and technical information (ages 11–18+)

English as a New Language
Early and middle childhood English as a new language (ages 3–12)
Early adolescence through young adulthood English as a new language (ages 11–18+)

English/Language Arts
Early adolescence English language arts (ages 11–15)
Adolescence and young adulthood English language arts (ages 11–18+)

Exceptional Needs
Early childhood through young adulthood exceptional needs specialist (ages birth–21+ years)

Generalist
Early childhood generalist (ages 3–8)
Middle childhood generalist (ages 7–12)
Early adolescence generalist (ages 11–15)

Library Media
Early childhood through young adult library media (ages 3–18+)

Mathematics
Adolescence mathematics (ages 11–15)
Adolescence and young adulthood mathematics (ages 14–18+)

Music
Early and middle childhood music (ages 3–12)
Early adolescence through young adult music (ages 11–18+)

Physical Education
Early and middle childhood physical education (ages 3–12)
Early adolescence through young adulthood physical education (ages 11–18+)

Science
Early adolescence science (ages 11–15)
Adolescence and young adulthood science (ages 14–18+)

Social Studies—History
Early adolescence social studies—history (ages 11–15)
Adolescence and young adulthood social studies—history (ages 14–18+)

World Languages Other Than English
Early and middle childhood world languages other than English (ages 3–12)
Early adolescence and young adulthood world languages other than English (ages 11–18+)

What Is the Basis for National Board Certification?

Standards for each discipline grow out of the NBPTS central policy statement, *What Teachers Should Know and Be Able to Do*. The vision of teaching this statement describes is based on five core propositions:

- Teachers are committed to students and their learning.

- Teachers know the subjects they teach and how to teach those subjects to students.

- Teachers are responsible for managing and monitoring student learning.

- Teachers think systematically about their practice and learn from experience.

- Teachers are members of learning communities.

In addition to these propositions, NBPTS certificates are structured around students' developmental levels and the subject(s) taught. For example, a teacher who is seeking early childhood certification is required to know the emotional, physical, and academic development representative of young children from birth through second grade. Each set of standards for a certificate represents consensus in the field of the critical aspects of teaching that distinguish the practice of accomplished teachers. Groups of teachers, teacher educators, developmental experts, and leaders in disciplinary fields work together until there is consensus on these standards. The proposed standards are then reviewed nationally and extensively before approval by the NBPTS board of directors. To become familiar with the standards, you might want to visit the National Board's web site, where they post the standards for each certificate area.

No certificate area is offered until this process is complete. This process can take up to several years, especially when it is difficult to reach consensus about the standards for a specific area. Additionally, certificate areas are reviewed periodically and changes are made with respect to assessment expectations. In fact, for the 2001 cycle all the certificate areas, except those that were new in 2000, were revised. The generalist certificates, being the oldest, underwent the most revision. The revision process has resulted in major changes in the portfolio process and in the assessment center expectations. Following are the new expectations:

- *Portfolio entries:* Teachers must submit four portfolio entries instead of six. Three of the entries are classroom-based and include two videos that document teaching practice and students' work. The fourth entry combines the teacher's work with students' families and community and collaboration with the professional community.

- *Assessment Center Entries:* There are six, thirty-minute assessment center prompts. These entries require a demonstration of knowledge of subject matter. Previously teachers were expected to do four, ninety-minute entries that combined pedagogical and content knowledge.

What Are the Rewards for National Board Certification?

National Board Certified Teachers often serve as role models and spokespersons for other teachers in the effort to build and to strengthen the teaching profession. They are examples of accomplished teachers, and they encourage others to complete the process. In some states and school districts, National Board Certified Teachers are called upon to provide advice, assistance, and mentoring to new teachers, student teachers, and experienced teachers seeking National Board Certification. They have been called upon to help inform educational policy decisions, and many National Board Certified Teachers are working in their districts or states to restructure curriculum, redesign school programs, and pilot test innovative teaching strategies.

Beyond these professional activities, teachers in most states are remunerated for their National Board Certified Teacher status. Some states even pay the fee for individual teachers to complete the process. Information for individual states, counties, and school districts is available at the National Board's web site and on states' web sites as well.

What Are the Connections Between Teachers Who Are Nationally Board Certified and Student Achievement?

A recent study was completed for the National Board by a research team from the University of North Carolina at Greensboro. The researchers sought answers to three questions (www.nbpts.org):

1. Do teachers certified by the NBPTS differ significantly from teacher candidates who did not earn certification in terms of the quality of their classroom teaching practices?

2. Do teachers certified by the NBPTS differ significantly from teacher candidates who did not earn certification in terms of the quality of work produced by their students on classroom assignments and on external modes of student assessment?

3. Do teachers certified by the NBPTS differ significantly from teacher candidates who did not earn certification in terms of their post-assessment professional activities?

For this study, sixty-five teachers were recruited from three geographic locations (North Carolina, Ohio, and Washington, D.C.). The research results indicate that, to a higher degree than noncertified teachers,

1. NBCTs possess those characteristics of expert teaching that have emerged from the body of research on teaching and learning.

2. NBCTs possess pedagogical content knowledge that is more flexibly and innovatively employed in instruction.

3. NBCTs are more able to improvise and to alter instruction in response to contextual features of the classroom situation.

4. NBCTs understand at a deeper level the reasons for individual student success and failure on any given academic task.

5. NBCTs' understanding of students is such that they are more able to provide developmentally appropriate learning tasks that engage, challenge, and intrigue students, but do not bore or overwhelm them.

6. NBCTs are more able to anticipate and plan for difficulties that students are likely to encounter with new concepts.

7. NBCTs are more able to generate accurate hypotheses about the causes of student success and failure.

8. NBCTs bring passion and deep commitment to their students' academic success to their work in classrooms.

9. NBCTs produce students who differ in profound and important ways from those taught by less proficient teachers. These students appear to exhibit an understanding of the concepts targeted in instruction that is more integrated, more coherent, and at a higher level of abstraction than understandings achieved by other students.

Achieving National Board Certification is a major accomplishment for a teacher that recognizes his or her exemplary teaching. This teaching is centered on students, curriculum, and the community. These teachers are able to demonstrate that they can teach to high standards, and as a result their students have higher achievement, among other benefits.

Program Support for Candidates

Although many teachers engage in this process alone, many states are urging candidates to work in support groups. Teachers pass at higher rates when they work in cohorts with a facilitator's support and guidance. Most facilitators participate in the facilitator training workshops provided by the National Board before taking on this leadership.

Of course, there is variability in the routines and expectations of cohort groups. I believe it would be helpful, though, to share some details of the support program in which I was involved so that teachers might see some of the benefits of this type of support. Our group began after teachers indicated their interest. Our collaborative meetings were scheduled on Saturdays throughout the school year. The goals of these meetings, which are similar to other support groups, were to provide emotional support, academic support, peer editing support for videos and entries, and resilience support so that all the candidates would complete the process. We held some celebrations as parts of the work were accomplished. We celebrated when the boxes were sent off to the Educational Testing Service and we celebrated when all the candidates completed the process.

When we began this process as a group, we were all pretty naïve about the expectations—not unusual for groups on their first attempt. I had gone to two workshops put on by the National Board to learn how to support candidates, although I had no experience doing this. We knew it would be labor and time intensive, but that is about all we knew. We began our work together by focusing on the materials in The Box, one section at a time. We began with the "Getting Started" section, which is included in every box. Following a review and discussion of this section, we talked about how important it was to be organized, to know the standards for each area, and to schedule when each entry would be finished.

At our first meeting, we listened and learned about each other as teachers. We worked through getting started. Most of the teachers had received their materials in the famous box and were now trying to figure out how to begin. Some teachers wanted to pursue one entry at a time, but they quickly found out that this would not be possible. Many of the entries required them to work with their students over time, so they needed to pursue these entries while they worked on others. These discoveries initially led to frustration, but then the teachers quickly resolved how they could work simultaneously on several entries and maintain their sanity.

Once everyone had a plan, we used our sessions to support each other, especially as individual teachers faced difficult life situations. For example, one teacher needed to support her husband as he went through cancer treatment. Another teacher suffered through what she described as a very difficult student teacher. And finally, one teacher broke her leg during the process. All these events consumed time and energy, but none of these teachers allowed them to be an excuse not to finish.

Other events stressed us all. Teachers talked about the videotaping process consistently. At first they were nervous about how to do the taping. They worried about what type of camera to use, what microphones would work best, and so on. These problems moved to the background of concern as they faced the videotaping itself. In some situations, their students became quiet, and froze in front of the camera. In other instances, they forgot to put a tape in the camera. When a teacher did get a video he or she was proud of, it was brought to the group for critical review. We watched the video to make sure that it accomplished what the National Board expected. Many sessions were spent evaluating videos for each other.

Through this process, we all learned about the exemplary teaching happening in our community. Applause and compliments were bestowed on all the teachers as they shared their videos. We were truly impressed with the quality of teaching we shared. We also learned about the daily dilemmas that many teachers faced; for example, small classrooms had too many students and classrooms were being painted in the middle of this process. Other teachers talked about students who worried them, and we all brainstormed possible solutions. Our group began to more fully understand teaching and learning from preschool to high school in a rich variety of settings.

One of the major causes of stress for the teachers was confirming that they followed all directions set forth by the National Board. A notice in the official materials said that failure to follow the directions would result in the entry's not being scored. So we spent time making sure that all directions were followed so every entry would be scored. This stress stayed with us until the final scores were distributed to each candidate. For this group of candidates, no one failed to have an entry scored because he or she did not follow directions.

The teachers talked about reflection as they participated in this process. They had thought they knew what that meant as a teacher, but now they really knew. One candidate said, "I used to think I knew why I was doing something with my students. Now I really reflect on why, and I often modify my plans because of that thinking." Another candidate said, "I knew I was a good teacher. My kids always did well on any sort of assessment. Now I know why my students are doing well. I understand how I was meeting their individual needs. This process made that clear to me."

We worked together throughout the entire academic year. We even met after most of the teachers had sent off their boxes in April; this is similar to the way other cohort groups work. We continued our work together for three reasons. First, we wanted to support the two candidates pursuing certificates in new areas. Their portfolios were not due until June. Second, we wanted to support each other as preparation was made for the assessment center. And third, we were used to supporting each other and we were not ready for the group to disband.

Once the teachers submitted their portfolios to the Educational Testing Service, each teacher prepared for the questions that might be asked at the full day of assessment center activities (They had to respond to four, ninety-minute exercises at the assessment center, requiring a whole day.). The National Board sent them materials to prepare for the assessment center. Some teachers received lists of books to read, and other teachers received a short list of what they might need to know. This group of teachers spent hours preparing for the four prompts that they would receive at the center.

Each candidate signed up for one full day at the center. (New candidates now spend only one half-day at the center.) They could bring reference materials to use while they worked, but everything they brought had to be written by them and destroyed when they left. Some teachers said they had time to refer to these prepared materials, but most said there just wasn't time. (Teachers now cannot bring in anything other than identification information.) Additionally, they learned that they could not reschedule these times, even when one candidate had the flu, and that they couldn't bring in even a tissue for a runny nose. It was no surprise that there was much stress related to this day of assessment.

When the teachers finished this day, the long wait began. It took until the end of November for the National Board to post the results. The National Board attempts to send a letter to each candidate with his or her results before names appear at its web site. Typically, after each teacher is notified by mail, it posts the results on the web site for anyone to see. For this very brave group of teachers, twelve passed on the first try—an amazing result. This was an incredible achievement; the pass rate for initial tries is about 35 percent to 45 percent. The teachers who finished in the first cohort represented elementary, middle, special education, and high school settings.

The results divided the support cohort into those who passed and those who did not on this first attempt. It was a difficult time for all of us. It was hard to celebrate when some of the group members had not been successful. This disequilibrium ended quickly though. We all celebrated, and then we got down to how we would support each other so that all members of this group would pass during the second year of the process. Teachers from the first cohort who did not pass on this first attempt are continuing the process. They can bank most of their scores and they will retake a few entries. These entries will be scored at the end of the year, and when these scores are combined with their banked scores, they should achieve the necessary score of 275 required for passing.

All support cohort groups face this difficult time because not every teacher in a group succeeds on the first try at this strenuous assessment. We found it important to figure out ways to support candidates as they retook parts of the process during the second year. This support varied for each teacher, based on self-identified needs. Some teachers elected to work with colleagues and others continued to work with the new cohort of candidates.

Final Thoughts

The process of National Board Certification allows teachers to demonstrate their exemplary abilities in the classroom. This certification allows quality teachers to remain in the classroom doing what they do best—teaching. Although these teachers might have chosen to become principals or to work in the central offices in their districts to be rewarded professionally, they can now remain in their classrooms and be rewarded. This is not to say that they may not seek other ways to work professionally; it just means that they are being rewarded for their teaching expertise.

As this group of exemplary teachers continues to grow, the results of their work will be more obvious to all. The expectation is that they will continue to teach and to positively affect the lives of more children, but they will also provide leadership to teachers and districts. Their work collectively and individually does and will continue to result in quality learning on the part of their students.

2

Reflections in a Human Mirror

Carol T. Hines

I couldn't breathe. My knees and arms felt detached and incapable of movement. I gasped for each breath in a near state of hyperventilation. I succumbed to a mouse-clicking frenzy trying to gain access to the long-awaited list of newly certified teachers on the NBPTS web site. Waves of anxiety swept over me when I thought of not certifying, while hints of euphoria offered hope that I would be listed among the names of the newly certified. A posting at *Talk to Other Teachers* had offered instructions on how to get to these results. I had to know. *Now!* I didn't want to receive an e-mail from someone with a message beginning, "Sorry to see you didn't certify." I just couldn't wait until I arrived home to discover my fate in the coveted privacy of the "Blue Room," my office. My first-period social studies class, at the middle school where I teach, would begin in less than fifteen minutes, and if I couldn't gain access to the results before then, I would have only snippets of time, except for my preparation period, to search for my name. The day's activities had me totally involved except for a few minutes at the beginning of each class. I had to know. *Now!*

I telephoned my husband, Brad, but reached only a recording of his voice. In my breathy message I explained that the results were posted on the Internet, and I provided him instructions for accessing the National Board's home page and locating the results. I encouraged, or rather begged, him to search for my name and let me know, either way. I told him I had to know.

Now! On my way to morning duty I visited briefly with Rick, a teacher down the hall, whose wife was in our cohort. I told him the results were posted on the Web, but not to tell me the results unless I had been certified.

I had time to try to log on to the site when I took attendance and when my classes quietly compared the bill of sale for a slave to that of a horse. After a long forty-five minutes, my second-period prep finally arrived and I clicked furiously for nearly forty minutes. No success. No e-mail arrived from Brad. The NB web site was ill equipped to handle thousands of instantaneous hits by anxious candidates. I joined the thousands of candidates hoping to turn this brief nightmare of waiting and not knowing into a dream come true.

Four hours later—an eternity—at the beginning of fifth period, I saw two e-mails from Brad. I took a deep breath and clicked on the first message, the mouse shaking in my sweaty palm. I couldn't open his attachment and he had not written a message. Unbelievable! My destiny so near yet so scrambled. I closed the file. My body literally quaked with each rapid pulse. I bordered on the dysfunctional in my frenzy to open the second message.

My National Board journey had begun eighteen months previously when the "Present Man," our pet name for the brown-clad UPS delivery person, delivered *The Box.* When the process ended I had invested a thousand hours in writing my six portfolios and had spent scores of hours preparing for six hours of exercises at the assessment center, which actually took ten hours to complete. Months passed as I reflected on my teaching until I resembled a human mirror. I ran out of words, yet I composed the best-written paragraphs of my life. I indulged in no movies and few dinners out for nearly eleven months. I consumed a forest of paper, a case of printer ink, and gallons of black coffee while discovering a person actually could survive for extended periods of time on four hours of sleep per night. I had waited patiently and anxiously for delivery of these coveted results for five and a half months, and now the answer was a mere mouse click away. Unbelievable! A rodent would deliver my destiny. At least I wouldn't have to wait for the blessed envelope. While simultaneously watching and avoiding the monitor screen, I commanded my finger to click the mouse and open Brad's message. Always a man of few words, he had simply written, "You got in. CONGRATULATIONS!!!!!!!!!!!!!!!"

An audible gasp shattered the silence of thirty thinking students. Tears channeled their way down my cheeks. A room of stunned and worried faces stared as I attempted composure.

"Are you all right, Mrs. Hines?" one student asked.

"Yes," I choked.

"But, you're crying!" they chorused.

"Good tears," I whispered pointing to my eyes. "These are good tears."

Through gentle sobs I told them that I just learned I had achieved my National Board Teaching Certificate as an Early Adolescent Generalist, and then I briefly explained what was involved and why this was so important to me. I had wanted to recluse myself to open that coveted envelope in private, but had I been informed through a letter I would have missed the music of students cheering, clapping, offering congratulations, and celebrating this monumental accomplishment. Their hurrahs, cheers, and shouts of, "You go, Mrs. Hines!" reaffirmed my decision and commitment to attempt National Board Certification to be the best teacher I could for my students. I was overwhelmed by the positive energy from my students colliding with my own joy. It was awesome!

I shared the good news with available staff at lunchtime and with students during my afternoon classes. More tears, hugs, and congratulations. It was wonderfully satisfying and emotional. Later I celebrated at home with my husband with an exquisite bottle of Navarro's Late Harvest Gewürztraminer and a greasy cheeseburger and fries. Life was good!

The next day when my fifth period came in they told me students had talked about seeing me crying in class yesterday. They said that other students had tried to guess why I was crying. The rumors were fabulous. They told me that some kids had said that I'd just heard my husband had broken both of his legs; others thought that something must have happened to Miss Scarlett, my yellow Lab puppy. Then one boy added, "Yeah, but Mrs. Hines, *we* knew the truth about what really happened!"

Twenty-four hours ago these students and I had shared something special when we celebrated my certification results. They reinforced my commitment to be the best teacher possible for the students who pass through my classroom on the way to their future.

In the Beginning

I was introduced to the National Board for Professional Teaching Standards (NBPTS) in November 1994, while attending a National Council for Social Studies Conference (NCSS) in Phoenix, Arizona. I visited with NBPTS representatives at their exhibitor's booth and they explained their program and commitment to teaching excellence. Stunned at the cost, I politely accepted their materials and promotional items and walked away. I remember that my colleague and I tried to figure out why a teacher would get a national teaching certificate, especially when it would cost you so much money. Besides, we already had teaching certificates from our state. Who needed two? We continued to stop by and chat at the NBPTS booth during biennial journeys to NCSS conferences. Little did I know that my attitude was to be readjusted permanently.

At the 1998 NCSS conference in Anaheim, California, I presented three workshops. A school district curriculum coordinator from Michigan who attended all three asked if I would present workshops for her district's elementary and middle school teachers. She was also interested in purchasing the educational materials I had co-written for use in my district and that were being used in districts and schools in other states, too.

I journeyed to Plymouth, Michigan, for two days of workshops in June 1999. Penny Joy, the Social Studies and Language Arts Curriculum Coordinator, asked if I was National Board Certified. I told her no, but that I was familiar with the organization. She said that she was a National Board Certified Teacher and that my teaching practice and pedagogy reflected the standards for teaching promoted by the NBPTS. She encouraged me to consider going through the process. Thus, my quest for National Board Certification was born.

In early July I requested information on the NBPTS through the Nevada State Education Association, which sent me a copy of NBPTS certificate overviews. As I read through the certificate description for Early Adolescent Generalist, I found a perfect fit. As I read each portfolio description, I knew exactly which lessons in my thematic units I would use for each of the four teaching-centered portfolios. I discussed this professional journey with my husband and decided National Board Certification was something I was going to achieve. I telephoned the office in San Antonio, Texas, where you pay for the testing, and by simply providing my credit card number I confirmed my commitment to this quest. Now I just waited for The Box to arrive. Subsequently, I learned that Nevada planned to offer financial incentives to assist with the cost of certification and to pay increases to certified teachers.

Washoe County School District and the University of Nevada, Reno (UNR), held an informational meeting for interested educators in early

September. I was the only person who had committed to the process and already had The Box. The attendees dwindled in number with each subsequent meeting. Our final cohort numbered nineteen teachers. Our facilitator, Dr. Diane Barone, with UNR, guided, cajoled, listened, encouraged, comforted, critiqued, motivated, and challenged us at our monthly meetings. All nineteen of us completed our portfolios and the assessment center exercises. She also orchestrated a wonderful reception for us at the university after our April deadline.

The Box

Cardboard is not an intimidating product; however, what lurked inside The Box would challenge, possess, and obsess me for the next nine months. I experienced a bit of a delay in getting started when I realized the standards I had been reading were for an Early Childhood, not Early Adolescent, Generalist. With a telephone call I ordered the correct standards; the delay provided me time to get acquainted with portfolio requirements and assessment protocols. *Tip:* Check and double-check the contents of The Box. Be certain that everything inside is for your certification area and is complete. *Tip:* Order an additional copy of your standards booklet. Amazingly, The Box and replacement standards booklet arrived before the extra copy I had ordered. Go figure!

I purchased colored folders so each portfolio and related materials would be easy to keep track of. Inside each folder I wrote notes and reminders of what I needed to do and keep, as well as pertinent dates. I also used colored paper for ease of organization—but then I color-coded everything.

I wrote lists and scoured files for documents to verify my school and professional accomplishments. I computer scanned and completed all forms and copied staff and student release forms, which I sent home after school started and the paperwork shuffle had eased somewhat, for both the parents and me. I kept all completed forms in separate folders and permission slips in their own folder.

I revised the order of items on my syllabus so that all my portfolio lessons and videotaping sessions would be completed by early February. I scheduled taping times with the school district's video center. Several friends spent many days in my classroom videotaping rehearsal tapes so that my students would feel more comfortable when the real tapings occurred. This was a very beneficial decision because my students ignored the district camera crew when it arrived and conducted class business as usual.

I hired our school's English aide, Doris, to proofread my writing for content, writing conventions, and so forth. She had read the NBPTS standards, portfolio requirements, and assessment guides. She designed a checklist for formatting page layout and content. I provided input and general rubric suggestions for her to use to double-check that I had followed all the directions and addressed all the requirements for each portfolio. Doris double read each entry, marking alternately in red and green ink. She checked off each question or item as she read the response. She wrote notes requesting clarification of my content. Doris checked to ensure all pages were labeled correctly and completely and that related housekeeping-type requirements were fulfilled. She provided an additional shoulder and/or ear when my stress levels soared, and rejoiced with me when I learned I had been certified.

As I completed each portfolio, I put it in The Box for safekeeping until it was time to pack it up and mail it off to the Lone Star State. The Box delivered me a challenge and I returned it with a full reflection of my teaching practice.

Processing Portfolios

I spent most of nine months planning, outlining, writing, and editing either at the computer or on the living room sofa. My housekeeper was cautioned not to disturb the piles of folders, books, and papers on the sofa or the stacks on the floor of the Blue Room, my office. My husband later christened the Blue Room the Soyuz 7 and the mouse my umbilical cord. He honestly believed that if I had had a hot plate or microwave and a coffeepot, I would never have left this capsule. He was probably right. I did remove my living room portfolio piles to the Blue Room over Christmas when I had sinus surgery. Drugs and discomfort forced me to put my quest on temporary hiatus.

After mid-January I awoke each weekday morning between two and three o'clock to review, revise, and write. A fresh pot of coffee kept me company as I proofed the typing from the previous evening, edited as needed, and refocused on the current portfolio. I wrote everything out in longhand, which frequently resulted in more arrows for added text than Cupid shoots on Valentine's Day! The physical act of writing kept me focused—something I don't get by typing as I write. That process just doesn't work for me.

Here's the visual:

I'm perched on an eight-foot fabric sofa in my nightie, a mug of hot coffee on the table within easy reach, and my left leg tucked underneath me. A portable writing desk rests on my lap. Stacks of colored folders and papers, pens, and pencils surround me. In close proximity are the handwritten bulleted standards. Bloom's vocabulary list sits next to the bulleted scoring guidelines and the binder that contains the written commentary guidelines. Early every morning I assumed the writing position and settled into the task at hand. When five o'clock arrived on school-day mornings, I returned everything to its proper stack and got ready for a day with students. On weekends I slumbered until seven or eight in the morning before I assumed the sofa or the typing position cocooned within my "Soyuz capsule."

Before I began a portfolio, I handwrote the standards in bulleted format to cement my focus. On a different shade of colored paper I bulleted the assessment criteria for a Level 4 only, the highest score on the rubric. For each portfolio entry, I highlighted the accomplishments and questions I needed to address. In the generous page margins I noted specific items for inclusion in my narrative. When writing, I kept a modified list of Bloom's taxonomy nearby so my language was as concise and descriptive as possible.

I tried to follow the suggested page length but juggled it to fit my writing needs. I knew how many words fit on a typed page, give or take a few. I further divided my writing allocations by how many areas I needed to address and the allowable total number of pages. I counted words more frequently than necessary; that's a common trait for those of us who are ADHD obsessive/compulsive, but this curse or blessing kept my writing tight and focused.

I saved all student work. Because my students usually complete portfolio assessments during the year, this was easy to do. However, I still had difficulty selecting students to focus on—students who had completed all assignments I planned to include and offered me adequate opportunity for analysis and reflection. My goal was to demonstrate that my teaching practice addressed the learning needs and styles of a diverse student population. For the Language Arts portfolio I selected a boy in Honors English and a girl in a regular English class. Both had the same English teacher. Their samples included a rapid writing activity, a draft only piece, and a writing web with a rough draft and final copy. These provided the most opportunity for analysis of the assignments, student work, and personal reflection. For the math portfolio, I selected three students—one in Honors math, one in middle school math, and one in remedial math. The girl in middle school math was also an English language learner student. Again, their diversity provided great opportunity for analysis and reflection. I followed the same format by selecting students representing various academic backgrounds for the other portfolio. I included special education students in my student mix. I had six social studies classes to select from but some classes were already being used with the videotapes or for another portfolio entry and I wanted to use students from all of my classes.

Specific Strategies

It took me some time to get organized and to develop strategies for completing all the entries for my portfolio. My strategies included the following:

- I finished one portfolio before beginning another. I needed to maintain that focus or else I'd have had none.

- I kept every handwritten and printed copy of each portfolio. I dated each copy for later reference if necessary.

- I labeled each portfolio section in bold caps. In some portfolios I typed each subsection or question in bold cursive and then did my writing. In other portfolios I stated the question in my first paragraph. However, I received higher scores on the portfolios with the subsection or questions typed in bold cursive.

- I didn't list my objectives or instructional goals in a consistent format. In some portfolios they were written as numbered items within the narrative. In other portfolios I bulleted the objectives or goals. Bulleting consumed more space but I feel it was more effective and it resulted in higher scores.

- When I analyzed student work, I used a rubric to record students' performance levels relative to the prompt to better evaluate their strengths and areas that needed more attention. I looked for perform-ance patterns to assist me in evaluating my teaching practice and the effectiveness of the prompts as learning and assessment tools. This format allowed me to assess how well students met the lesson objectives and the areas that needed remediation.

- I tried to create or imagine the rubric I would design to evaluate the objectives for each portfolio as if I were the assessor. I used a similar graphic organizer when I analyzed student responses to a prompt. This ensured that I addressed all areas for each student.

- Sometimes I inserted my standards as I wrote; other times I annotated my standards after I finished the written commentary. I removed the parentheses for added space. I kept a tally of the times I addressed each standard to see if I adequately demonstrated my teaching practice. Annotating the standards after I finished writing was easier and, I feel, more effective. This practice helped me to evaluate how clear, concise, and convincing my evidence was.

- I scripted my videos verbatim. I watched each video without sound to observe body language. I even encouraged my assessors to give the video a replay without the sound and to watch the students' interac-tions, which were incredible! I wrote out the questions each video needed to address and answered these as I watched the video. I identi-fied the students by number both in my narrative and on the class-room layout page. I thought this format would make it easier for my assessor. I transferred each twenty-minute segment onto three video-cassettes—one to send, one in my emergency reserve box, and one backup for me in addition to the full-length original. I taped for real on only two occasions, three to four classes each time. There was one taping session for each video portfolio. I selected the best twenty-minute segment and described what had happened before and after. This resulted in excellent scores including one 4.25.

- A few students addressed me by name during a taping and mentioned our state. I still used the video even though teachers are expected to mask their identity and the identity of their state. These minor slips of the tongue were overshadowed by the quality of the taping. I did remove some identifying items from display in my classroom (e.g., felt maps of Nevada made by my students). But, I left up other items and all my paraphernalia and decorations for the Green Bay Packers. The assessors would think I was either from Nevada or Wisconsin, though I've never had the pleasure of visiting the latter.

• For documented accomplishments relating to professional growth and outreach to school and community, I organized my evidence in the following order: School, Community, District, State, and National. I discussed my accomplishments and then provided the evidence. I did not use the continuous narrative format. I used a combination of verification forms and actual artifacts. I tried to be very specific in relating my accomplishments to student learning and not merely student impact. This also relates to the contact log. I wrote about how the contact affected student learning. In my interpretive summary I discussed the patterns of my accomplishments and collaborations in clear and concise language and related how they build and benefit students' learning in my classroom and ultimately the students in the classrooms of other teachers by providing convincing evidence here. I showed the significance of the accomplishment, how it relates to or impacts my teaching practice, and then I connected it to student learning. I stressed the quality of my accomplishment, why it's important, and how it benefited my teaching practice and student learning. Some of my interpretive summaries were only one-half page and others required a full page. I justified each accomplishment by answering the questions, why do this and what will this affect? I was succinct but thorough in my writing: clear, concise, and convincing.

• By the time I was finished writing my portfolios, I felt quite full of myself. This is no time for professional modesty, however; discreet bragging and boasting is now in order. I needed to address specifically what I do in my teaching practice that makes it successful. I explained why and how what I do benefits student learning.

Bon Voyage, My Cardboard Friend

It was around ten o'clock at night on Saturday, April 8. Adrenaline raced through my body with each rapid heartbeat. The light at the end of my tunnel grew brighter. My fingers flew across the keyboard in rapid staccato. I typed the final words, clicked the Save icon, then Print, and sat back. My body quaked in a shudder as tears welled in my eyes. It was over. I was finished. This part of my journey toward National Board Certification had ended. Relief, sadness, and pride collided with other emotions. I felt everything and nothing. The ending of my quest had been nearly as overwhelming as the beginning.

Packing the pages of pulpy prose that represented nine months of my life, my teaching practice, and soulful reflection proved an exercise in logistics and stamina. I spent an entire day assembling the contents of The Box. This envelope. That portfolio. Double-check that the videos were cued to view and inserted in the correct envelope. Paper clip this. Paper clip that. This envelope goes first and that one goes last. I checked and double-checked the order of the contents and asked Brad for a third inspection. Once assured that everything was dotted, crossed, labeled, and identified with my personal number, I ceremoniously lowered the lid and turned the light out on this phase of the certification process. After some redundant taping to secure my precious cargo on its journey to Texas, The Box was ready for sending.

I bid The Box a tearful farewell Monday morning. My husband was delivering it to the custody of Federal Express for its trip to San Antonio. He had his instructions for the clerk on what they could and could not do to The Box. Because I was leaving town on Wednesday to present workshops and attend a regional social studies conference, I had a second complete box ready for mailing, sans the official envelopes of course, in case The Box didn't arrive in San Antonio by Wednesday. I was taking no chances at this point. I even considered flying to Denver via San Antonio to deliver The Box in person.

Brad e-mailed me the Federal Express tracking number at school, and I began tracking my box's journey. I tracked The Box from Reno to Tennessee to Texas. At 10:23 A.M. on Tuesday, April 11, The Box was safely delivered and signed for at the NBPTS office in San Antonio. Relief! What a wonderful emotion.

General Strategies and Tips

- Hire a housekeeper.

- Apply for an extension on your income taxes. The "T" word was not allowed to be spoken in my home until after my day at the assessment center.

- Visit the NBPTS Web site.

- Link to *Talk to Other Teachers.* Ask specific questions for your area of certification. Always post your certificate area and the portfolio you need help with. To get the best response, be concise in your inquiries.

- E-mail questions to the National Board for clarification when needed. Go to the source and get the NB's response in writing.

- Join an e-group or visit one of the many chat rooms for your certification area.

- Find a colleague in your certification area to work or chat with. I had no one, and it's lonely at times.

- Join a cohort. Take whatever support you can get—emotional, professional, and mental. My cohort was tremendously supportive. I enjoyed meeting and working with our diversified community.

- Find someone to read and edit for you. Pay him or her if necessary. Other people's time has a value, too.

- Save everything to disk, one for each portfolio; but make sure you do it right. Label the disks.

- Check to see that the backup files option on your computer is turned on. Set it for automatic save every two minutes or less.

- Save copies of everything, just in case.

- E-mail a copy of your portfolio files to your school's computer. If your computer crashes or you lose a disk, you'll know where to access a copy of your work.

- Write tight. Toss out those *be* verbs whenever possible. They waste space and inspire less descriptive and concise writing. Make every word count. They do!

- Know how many words and rows fit on a full page and a half-page. Outline the different areas you write about in each portfolio and decide how many words or pages is allotted. I recommend reserving a full page for all reflections. I sometimes needed more, which meant less space for something else.

- Use headers and footers.

- Check and double-check your page setup to guarantee you meet the layout requirements.

- Write out the videotaping requirements for whoever is manning the camera. Each portfolio is different and you want each video session to be eligible for inclusion.

- Know your standards.

- Ask your school or parent group for financial assistance to pay the cost of National Board Certification. The parent group at my school gave me $500 toward the fee.

- Color-code everything.

- Buy printer ink and paper when it's on sale.

- Plan the teaching year day by day before the year begins in the fall. My thematic teaching unit packets were completed and sent to the district's print shop before school started. Fortunately, few changes were necessary during the year. Prior planning and streamlining really paid off.

- Take vitamins. Exercise. Eat. Sleep. Make time for romance. Do all in moderation. The days pass too quickly and you will be mailing The Box to San Antonio before you know it.

Glitches, Pratfalls, and Murphy's Law

When I reflected on my experiences with the National Board Certification process, I created a list of some of my most interesting incidents. Some of these centered on writing entries and others concerned my health. Here's a list I eventually labeled "Glitches, Pratfalls, and Murphy's Law."

- I ran out of words, literally. It was horrible. I collected every thesaurus in the house. My husband even offered vocabulary options. I could describe the word I needed but the actual word evaded me.

- I spent two hours editing out eight words to meet the page limit of a portfolio. "Write tight" acquired a new definition.

- When printing the final portfolio copies for packing, I opened the science portfolio file. The screen lied to me, and my computer reflected a demented side by displaying the math portfolio. I closed that file and clicked to open the science file. Math again. I opened the science disk. Math! I opened the math file and disk and found math. My science file was *gone*! My science portfolio had disappeared. I panicked. I couldn't breathe. I shook, gasped, and cried uncontrollably. I would have to retype the entire science portfolio. Of course, I hadn't yet printed a hard copy of the final version of this particular portfolio. Brad came in and found me crumpled and crying on the verge of hysteria. He's not just a man of few words, but also methodical. He asked questions and I shuddered responses. He searched the hard drive. *No science.* Because he was the only rational person around, he remembered that I had e-mailed some of the portfolio entries to my school computer. Was it possible that one of those was science? I opened my school e-mail and there it was. I forwarded it to myself at home. I blessed and paid homage to all techno-nerds everywhere who had anonymously made this technology a reality.

- I had sinus surgery in December and planned to write and reflect over Christmas vacation. Age slows the healing process, as does an anesthesiologist who pinged a nerve not once but twice in the same spot on my right wrist. I couldn't write without my arm and hand reacting as if I'd stuck a wet finger in a wall socket. Hand rest and drug therapies were prescribed but the drugs were a bit too mind-altering and I couldn't think to write a complete sentence, let alone reflect. I discontinued the drugs and finally, by the end of January, my mental faculties returned. The length of time I can use my hand and arm continue to be limited. This difficulty belabored this process and ultimately exacerbated my current condition.

- On March 1, I fell off a platform-type step while out of town working on the writing team for the new state standards for social studies. Witnesses said I was unconscious for more than ten minutes. I flew home after a visit to an emergency clinic. I couldn't move for several days. The doctor said my fall was equal to being hit by a vehicle on only the right side of my body. Now I had new aches and pains to join the electrical stimulation in my right hand and arm. Physical therapy three times per week for more than two hours, plus at-home exercises, were consuming what little time I wasn't allocating to the National Board. These were now longer days and even shorter nights.

- The only slot available for my certification area at the assessment center was on the last full day of school with students. I was incensed. I wrote to the National Board relating what I had to complete before June 6 and the unfairness that Early Adolescent Generalists had little or no after-the-school-year time to prepare for the Center. The National Board agreed and arranged for a new date the following week, yet still within the testing window and at no cost to me.

The Assessment Center

After sending off my portfolio, I prepared for the assessment center. The following list of strategies was helpful during preparations.

- Schedule your time as soon as you receive your packet.

- Read and study the materials provided.

- Make lists of sample lessons that could apply.

- Review appropriate course content.

- Reread Piaget and take notes. I hadn't been in a classroom, as a student, for twenty-nine years. This was an excellent refresher.

- Read and review texts from related core areas.

- Prepare the materials you would take if you could and use those for study purposes.

- I wrote brief notes to my assessor about what I thought or how an activity matched one of my own. I even critiqued the exercises. The one I scored lowest on was the one I criticized most; however, I don't believe my honesty affected my score. I just didn't adequately demonstrate what was required.

- Visit the testing center prior to your test date. Take a tour and plan your travel route.

- Sleep well the night before.

- Get up a little earlier than necessary so you won't feel rushed.

- Arrive before your scheduled time.

- Leave snacks and water in a cooler in your car.

- Between exercises leave your cubicle and walk around. Clear your head and prepare for your next exercise. Breathe!

- Take notes on your prompts before you begin typing. This helps you to focus on the current exercise. Focus, focus, focus! Be clear, concise, convincing!

- When I finished at the assessment center, I had no memory of my first three exercises. Hours passed before I remembered what they were and the order in which I had completed them. That was my level of focus.

- If you are distracted or disturbed by *any* conditions or individuals, speak up immediately and insist the conditions be remedied at once. My proctor was engaged in a boisterous conversation in the windowed observation room. I promptly walked over, opened the door, and politely but emphatically told him he had to take his conversation elsewhere, and that I wouldn't allow him to disturb my concentration and influence my testing conditions. He apologized and I completed my exercises in silence, except for the clicking of a keyboard. Be assertive and your own advocate if necessary.

Impact on My Teaching Practice

I truly enjoyed my pursuit of National Board Certification. As I progressed through the portfolios, I found that I was adjusting my attitude, seeing my students differently, and tweaking my curriculum to better meet the needs and learning styles of my students. Analyzing their work and committing the videos to memory provided an insight that had been missing in my teaching practice and assessment of students' learning. I looked at my students more holistically. I got rid of teacher baggage that I'd acquired over the years. With my renewed teaching synergy, I experienced a "what luck!" feeling comparable to finding Ed McMahon at my front door with a check to finance my future. Pedagogy began to resemble a chameleon, and I liked what I saw.

This year is fantastic. I incorporated the projected changes I wrote about in my portfolios. What a difference they made for my students. I streamlined lessons to add focus. The revised writing prompts in my Slavery, Orphan Train, and Famous African Americans mini-unit produced very thoughtful and reflective student poetry. Students wrote powerful words on these subjects. A more concise format for my Archaeology Dig unit provided deeper understanding of the scientific method. It's exciting, stimulating, and rewarding for all of us. When assessing how my students are learning, I listen now with my eyes and not just my ears. This provides a new perspective to my teaching practice, and I like how it looks and feels.

I've relinquished control and the belief that my ideas alone should be used. That was my arrogance. My Teacher Power. I volleyed this power back to my students. Student-created projects and assessment rubrics have empowered them to learn in their style, not mine. This results in more energized and motivated students performing at levels I previously only dreamed about. They are creating multilevel projects and grading rubrics. We're all excited, stimulated, and rewarded with this process. I'm rapidly becoming an authentic facilitator in my students' learning quest. We are all flourishing with the results of my attitude readjustment.

My curriculum is more focused and purposeful. Students are making their own connections as to how the things we do in my class will benefit them in other classes and in their future. This is in part due to Action Research and changing my portfolio assessment format so that my students learn to make these connections through their own reflection. I reflect on all my teaching and my students' learning. In return, my students reflect on their personal learning and help me adjust my teaching. That mirror thing is everywhere now, and I like traveling in this new direction.

I am a better student of my students' learning styles, limitations, and strengths. My immersion in their work last year opened a whole new spectrum for teaching, assessing, and understanding my students as learners.

I am as busy as ever with new opportunities coming my way. National Board Certification opened the door for me to grow, share, and participate in teaching and learning in unexpected and wonderful venues. What I thought was the ride of my life was only the first curve in many tomorrows to come. I am holding on tight for whatever the future brings my way.

Support Through the Whole Process: The Nitty-Gritty Issues

Diane Barone with National Board Teachers and Candidates

As teachers consider the process required for certification by the NBPTS, they are frequently overwhelmed by the enormity of the task at hand. Often they have second thoughts as they investigate what is required and how they might even know that. The infamous Box arrives and is filled with directions, very specific directions, and it is often frustrating for teachers to determine where to begin. To help teachers work through this process, we have broken it down into its component parts and provided suggestions and examples of strategies that were used by teachers working toward National Board Certification.

This chapter is organized around specific requirements and tasks. It begins with the decision and what a teacher, perhaps you, might consider before saying yes or no. Following this discussion, we address time management, support communities, portfolio construction, videotaping, and writing. The chapter ends with preparation for the assessment center and waiting for results.

Throughout this chapter you will hear the voices of National Board teachers and candidates. Their words come from oral and written conversations where they reflected on the certification process.

The Big Decision

For some teachers, the decision to pursue National Board Certification is the hardest part of the process. In general, teachers who elect to be a candidate for National Board Certification are already very busy with their teaching. If they determine they are ready to engage in the certification process, it means finding 200 to 400 additional hours in their schedules. For some teachers, this is the deciding factor; they either can or cannot find the time to complete the requirements of the process in a satisfactory manner.

If you are a teacher who is planning to engage in the National Board Certification process, critically analyze your schedule: Can you find blocks of time to work on the portfolio entries and to prepare for the assessment center? This is a question that only you can answer, and it is an important one. Beyond this question, it is probably not a good idea to enter this process if you are getting married, divorced, or having a baby during the year. Additionally, if you have just been elected to a major leadership role in your school, district, or state, it is probably not the best time. However, we have learned that there is never a perfect time to go through National Board Certification. Life does not stand still just because you have decided to engage in this process; children will still be sick, your class may not be the easiest you have ever had, and other issues might make the challenge of the process more difficult. Although the circumstances may be very difficult, they do not decrease your chances to be certified. They just mean that you need to adjust and continue the process while handling difficulties.

All kinds of teachers enter this process. Some have just completed their first three years of teaching and others are at the end of their careers. Each teacher is still faced with the difficult decision surrounding the National Board assessment process. Jessica Daniels, a National Board teacher, talks in a humorous way about teachers who might choose to become a National Board teacher. She writes:

To enter into the National Board process, you should be an educator who is already overworked and whose plates of projects, demands, and obligations are completely full. If you are a teacher who is prepared to pull information from as deep as your furthest toenail, search every last brain dendrite, regurgitate rhetorical reflection, and bleed on paper, then this is right for you.

As her writing about the National Board process continues, she provides a survey for potential candidates to complete. You may want to complete her survey to help with your decision (see Figure 3.1). If your answers are mainly yes, then she concludes that you have the "guts, fortitude, and caring heart" that represent a National Board Certified Teacher, and you should say yes.

Figure 3.1

Decision Survey

1. Do you skillfully balance your number one priority, family, with your love of teaching and learning?
2. Do you take on more responsibilities and juggle multiple, simultaneous demands with ease?
3. Are you a teacher who is always available and you know the door to your class revolves, because you are never alone?
4. Are you a teacher who constantly has someone in the room seeking, needing, sharing, or exchanging?
5. Are you the role model who wears any hat needed, from the shining-moments sponsor to the understanding tear wiper?
6. Are you the resource and sounding board for collegial questions, the mentor ready with words of support and uplifting validations, and the manager making hundreds of decisions daily?
7. Are you the colleague whose wisdom stems from your ability to listen?
8. Are you there before and long after the school day ends?
9. Do your students comment on how innovative, creative, and dedicated to the art of teaching you are?
10. Do you encourage parents to be active participants in their children's learning?
11. Are you a teacher who is so positive you don't notice if a glass is half full or half empty? You only care that it will hold liquid and is recognized as being full of potential.

Another National Board teacher, Jeanine VanDeVort, used her computer to make her decision. She went to her favorite search engine to find out all she could about the National Board. She wanted to consider this process beyond what might be written on the National Board's web site. She found detailed information and personal accounts from other teachers on becoming a National Board Certified Teacher. She describes how she wanted to join this group of committed teachers after "reading the personal stories of motivation and commitment shared by them." Although Jeanine was certified in her first attempt at this process, she also learned that for most teachers it takes two or three years to become certified. She commented that while she knew this fact, she didn't focus on it at all as she went through the process. She says, "I just couldn't wait to get started."

Finally, before making a decision to engage in this rigorous process, it is important to explore fully the core propositions of the National Board. Brainstorm how you demonstrate each of the core propositions. Be specific. What exactly do you do? If your principal or another teacher came to visit and observe in your classroom, what would he or she see that would demonstrate your teaching in relation to the core principles that follow?

1. Teachers are committed to students and their learning.

2. Teachers know the subjects they teach and how to teach those subjects.

3. Teachers are responsible for managing and monitoring student learning.

4. Teachers think systematically about their practice and learn from experience.

5. Teachers are members of learning communities.

You now have a basic idea of the energy and time commitment required of this process. You know where to find information about the process. You have critically looked at who you are as a teacher and how you operationalize the National Board core propositions. So you are now ready to make your decision and consider the specific requirements of the assessment process. One of the first things to determine is the right certificate area for you. After reading the chapter by Leo McBride, you will understand that selecting the right area is not always a straightforward task. As more certificate areas become available, however, this task becomes easier.

Managing Time

The biggest concern for teachers who attempt the National Board assessment process is managing time because this process requires a huge time commitment. The most successful strategy that we discovered is to work backwards. Currently, due dates are variable and depend on the certificate that is chosen. For example, during the year that a new certificate becomes available, it is not sent to teachers until December. Those teachers then have a June deadline. Teachers who receive their portfolio materials sooner typically have an April due date.

Once the portfolio's due date was established, the teachers in our cohort immediately worked back two weeks for their completion deadline. By moving the date back, the teachers had a reduction in tension because they had built in time to pack up their materials and deal with any last-minute changes. Petrina McCarty commented that "This gave me some flex time in case I fell behind schedule; I could still get it in on time."

You may be wondering why a candidate would want to leave time for packing and potential revision. We weren't sure that this was necessary when we started the process, but it was essential for the majority of candidates. Perhaps Jeanine VanDeVort describes it best in her reflection of the process:

> It took me three hours to pack The Box! Portfolios covered the pool table and table tennis table in our game room. Before any portfolio was sealed for the last time and placed in The Box to be mailed out, it would have to go through one final scrutiny. I made sure that each form from the forms envelope was correctly in place. The knowledge that if anything was left out, the portfolio might not be scored was a constant song that ran through my head. It seemed every time I checked a portfolio, I would find something that was not quite right or missing. In the Outreach to Families and Community and Professional Development entry, I found that I had neglected to put labels with my I.D. number on a few. Next, I found a form that was not in the right place. I remember thinking that I would probably not pass because I was too dumb to pack The Box right. Finally, though, I could find nothing wrong with any of the portfolio entries. I sealed The Box shut.

You may be thinking that you will never be as stressed as Jeanine was, but you most likely *will* be. Packing The Box is a very detailed process and it comes at the end of the assessment work, when you are tired. There are very specific directions for each entry and the way it must be compiled. These rules exist so that the scorers see the same format for each entry and scoring is accomplished easily and equitably for all teachers. However, knowing this does not make dealing with the details less frustrating. Perhaps the most important detail is that the entry in each envelope must match the title on the envelope. Each entry is sent to different scorers, each of whom is responsible for only one entry. If the wrong entry is placed in an envelope, then that entry will be scored according to the expectations of a different entry. For example, if the Parent Communication and Professional Development entry is placed in the Student Learning envelope, it will be scored as though it were the Student Learning entry. So packing is important.

Each year, several teachers who have not built in this time accompany their boxes on a plane to San Antonio to meet the deadline. More than a hundred teachers did just that this past year. You will not have to do this if a few weeks of cushion time are built into your schedule.

Once the two-week cushion is planned, each entry needs a time frame. Allowing one month per entry seems to work quite well; however, in most circumstances you will be working on more than one entry at a time. The month-per-entry plan allows enough time for completion and any revision that might be necessary. Once your schedule is complete, post it at school and above the computer that you will be working on, so that you are constantly reminded of deadlines.

Most teachers start first on their Parent Communication and Professional Accomplishments entry. These entries require gathering information and verification from many sources. By starting early, teachers have a large pool of choices and are not stressed when one letter or verification form does not come or is not adequate for the process.

More will be said later about videotaping classroom practice, but starting to videotape early is critical to success in this process. Most teachers find it better to have several videos to choose from, rather than scheduling only one or two sessions for videotaping and then finding the video is not of the quality necessary for this process.

Time management also means finding consistent time and a regular place to work on the portfolio entries. Two teachers, Ginny Beck and Carol Hines, found it easiest to get up early each morning and work before setting off to school. They spent the rest of their day focused on the teaching and learning that occurred in their classroom. Other teachers blocked the weekends to work, and they did work all day Saturday and Sunday through most of the process. This meant that school work, family time, social engagements, and so on were all modified for this schedule.

Along with planning time and setting a schedule, finding a location for this process is essential. Each teacher identified a place in his or her home where all the pieces and papers surrounding the National Board assessment process were placed. To keep track of the pieces and papers, each teacher created an organizational system. Many bought colored folders, one color for each entry. They also used highlighters, colored tabs, and Post-it notes to keep the materials organized. And they usually had a rule that no one in their household could touch these materials.

A Support Community

Before tackling the specifics of the portfolios, I would like to highlight the importance of a community to support you in this process. Certainly, teachers can engage in the National Board assessment alone and be successful, although the rate of this success is very low, generally less than 20 percent.

One teacher in our cohort, Margaret Thiel, talked often of the importance of a support group. For this she had to drive 300 miles each way to be a part of a community of teachers. She provides an overview of the support group throughout the entire process:

> The friendship and supportiveness shown to each of us was invaluable. We were able to discuss the difficulties we were having, commiserate about our hectic schedules, and laugh about the funny things that were happening to us as we did our entries. It was great to hear about the fire drill that happened just before the entry was being videotaped, and about one teacher who had a student arrested while filming his lesson. We got to see wonderful teachers in action, and we were glad to see that unforeseen problems crop up in everyone's days.

In my work with National Board teachers and from other groups of teachers going through this process, I hear that the teachers find support from others critical to their success. Support groups come in all kinds of forms. In some school districts, such as Los Angeles, the school district and teachers' association provides support for candidates, who also receive support from the state. In other locations, such as Idaho, the support might be grant-based. Some universities provide this support as well. In some cases, like mine, the university provides a class to support teachers. In other places, the university may have developed a whole master's program for this support. There are support groups in almost every community, and others can be formed. This information is usually available at a state department of education web site.

The role of the support group is to do just that—support each candidate through the process. The group works together to answer questions as they arise. The members critique each other's videos and written entries before they are complete. They ensure that each teacher has documented his or her teaching to the standards and has done this *clearly, consistently, and convincingly*. The support group is there to lend emotional support as well. When a video is a disaster or a teacher has a family emergency, the group listens and sometimes helps. And it also celebrates accomplishments such as sending The Box, completing the assessment center activities, and becoming a National Board Certified Teacher.

What I have discovered about these groups is that they continue to exist after the process is complete. Through the close work required during the assessment process that opens up a teacher's classroom to colleagues, they form professional bonds that continue after the work is done.

Beyond this support group, teachers often form smaller groups based on certificate area. When these groups meet, they can focus on the specific requirements of their certificate area. Other small groups might consist of colleagues who teach in the same school. They can meet informally and work on portfolio entries together.

Many teachers also secure the help of other teachers, friends, and sometimes copy editors to help with specific requirements. Often these folks come in and videotape for a teacher or are willing to critically read an entry and provide feedback based on the expectations of the entry. This feedback is important when a teacher finds that he or she is too close to what has been videotaped or written to critically analyze it and compare it to the standard requirements. This new perspective often makes the entries richer in detail and makes sure that no standard is missing in the write-up.

The Portfolio Entries

Each certificate area requires four portfolio entries. Each entry requires a teacher to document that he or she can teach to the National Board standards. The specific standards that need to be addressed in each entry are identified. These vary by certificate area and the National Board provides a standards book for each candidate that details each standard. Moreover, each entry has very specific directions as to length of the written commentary, whether a video is required and its length, and what kinds of student work or artifacts are required. The directions for each entry are very specific, and there is a graphic organizer to help a candidate know what is expected. The National Board also helps candidates by providing a "Making Good Choices" section in each entry. This section is important for candidates to consider because it provides suggestions and guidance for the choices a candidate must make. And most important, in all the decisions a teacher makes, he or she must tie all evidence to *student learning*. These ties are critical and must be explicit. As a teacher writes an entry, he or she needs to constantly consider why and how this was important to student learning. "Student learning" has become the mantra in all my work with candidates. Without evidence of it, an entry is not complete and requires revision until student learning is highlighted. This is true for all entries, even the one that is not classroom-based.

Family and Community Outreach Entry

Each entry, three of which are classroom-based, has a different purpose. The fourth entry is a combination entry in which a teacher is expected to document his or her work with families, the community, colleagues, and the teaching profession. For this entry, teachers reflect on the work they routinely do with parents and the community. They collect evidence of this work and seek verification from those most directly affected by it. Candidates think about what they do in their classrooms, schools, communities, states, and, where appropriate, at the national level.

To document family communication, teachers are expected to complete a communication log. Figure 3.2 is a sample communication log completed by a National Board teacher. Beyond the log, teachers include letters from teachers and students. Jeannine Paszek included a letter from a student to demonstrate her work with families (see Figure 3.3).

Figure 3.2

Documented Accomplishments II.
Outreach to Families and Community Communication Log

Accomplishment No. _____   Candidate ID _____

Date	Person Contacted	Type of Communication (Telephone, Written, E-mail, or in Person)	Nature of Communication (Reason for Communication, Outcome of Communication)
01/04/00	Tyler's mom	In person	Tyler and his mother came in to discuss the problems Tyler was having with math. She asked me to help him. I agreed. She went to work and I tutored Tyler.
01/05/00	Marlana's mom	Written	I sent a note home to Marlana's mom applauding Marlana's excellent behavior and work ethics. Marlana has been a model student since we returned from Christmas break.
01/05/00	Sean's mom	Written	A note was sent home requesting a conference to discuss Sean's behavior in class. It highlighted several classroom and playground incidents where he has been bothering other students.
01/06/00	Matthew's mom	In person	We discussed Matthew's lackadaisical attitude toward his written work. I shared several copies of sloppy, illegible work. We discussed possible solutions and set some logical consequences for a lack of effort.
01/06/00	Troy, Andy, Julie, and Elaine; grade-level meeting	In person	We discussed an upcoming field trip, fundraising ideas, study hall/detention, cooperative scheduling, and year-round school issues. We will meet again next month. Copied minutes to principal.
01/07/00	Steve, vice principal	In person	Met to discuss upcoming evaluation and scheduled a visitation time. Discussed paperwork and procedures.
01/07/00	Sean's mom and Sean	In person	Discussed Sean's behavior in class. Outlined some logical consequences for future misbehavior. Sean's mom agreed and requested a weekly progress report be sent home on Fridays.

Figure 3.3

> Mrs. Paszek :~
>
> I can't believe it's already over. It's time for me to move on and finally go out into the real world. Thanks to great teachers like you, I'm not too worried, I feel very confident. Do you remember 1° Science Inquiry in 1996? I sure do, I'll never forget it. That was the first year I ever got an A in any kind of science class. You have taught me how to enjoy science and chemistry rather than just getting it done for an A. I have to say that in my 4 years of attending Galena, I've had many great teachers, but you are without a doubt, my favorite. Thank you for opening my eyes and believing in me, even when I didn't. I wish you many more wonderful years in teaching, as for me, maybe someday you'll see me on Dateline!
>
> P.S. See you at   Yours truly,
> graduation!
>
> *Erica La Jaunie*
>
> Class of 2000!

Cora Carrigan, a National Board teacher in English as a New Language, found the task of getting verification forms particularly difficult. Her students and their parents spoke and wrote minimally in English. She chose to meet individually with parents; she talked to them in their home language and explained that she needed them to comment on the tutoring she engaged in with students outside of school hours. They stated what they wanted to say in their home language. Cora translated it to English and dictated the letters and words they should make to convey this message in writing (see Figure 3.4).

Figure 3.4

Verification Form

This form is especially interesting because Cora had to translate to the parents what she was writing. Then she had to help them write their response in English. Cora works with parents and children for whom English is a new language. The verification forms need to be completed in English, so this is how Cora solved this dilemma.

Candidate Name: ___Cora L. Carrigan_____

Below, briefly describe the accomplishment(s) being verified by the signer of the form. Explain **what** the accomplishment is and **why** it is noteworthy.

At times, ESL students need additional tutoring instruction which they cannot receive during regular school hours. When the situation warrants intense instruction, I make arrangements with parents for their children to come to school during vacation time. I do this because I enjoy working with my students and it gives me a great deal of pleasure to see them make strides academically. If a child cannot come in during vacation, I tape record books and loan materials to the families so their children's progress does not suffer. As I tape the books, I use the child's name throughout the story. This personalization prevents the students from becoming bored and holds their interest. Students and parents appreciate my personal interest and I enjoy helping my students develop a life-long interest in reading.

(To be completed by the verifier after the candidate has completed the top section.)

Is the candidate's description of his or her activities accurate?

____✓____ Yes   _____ No   _____ Don't Know

How do you know of these activities?   Mrs, Carrigan has, given my son, Jose a los of e$Tra help. He is doing well

Signature: _Veronica Ramos_____

Name (please print): _VeRonicA Ramos_____ Date: _4 - 7 - 00____

Title or Position: _MOTHER_____

A final example of this documentation comes from Barbara Surritte, who asked her principal to document her work in a reading club for students. In Figure 3.5, she explains why she chose this activity for her entry and gives an example of the documentation that she submitted, which included the note from her principal and an agenda from one meeting of the club.

The Family and Community Outreach entry was often difficult for teachers to complete. They were reluctant to share the work they did with parents and professionals because they felt it was boasting. We worked through this issue, as have other National Board candidates; this is the time to boast and brag about the work that you do with families and professionals. This work does make a difference to the learning of students in the classrooms of National Board teachers and candidates, and it should be recognized. One way to do this is to document it in this entry.

Classroom-Based Entries

Three entries are based in each teacher's classroom. Two of these entries require the teacher to videotape lessons and student interaction. The third entry has the teacher evaluating student work. These three entries have the most weight assigned to them in the scoring process. They are considered the most authentic measure of a teacher's ability.

For these entries, it is critical that the teacher select examples of his or her teaching practices that represent the whole of his or her teaching. Each video is a small sample of a teacher's repertoire, and it will be judged against the standards. Many of the teachers used Bloom's taxonomy to help them select lessons. They wanted lessons that represented the highest levels on this taxonomy (see Figure 3.6).

For the student work entry, making good selections is equally important. A teacher needs to choose two students, compare the knowledge they have demonstrated, and determine how future lessons will be built on this knowledge. It requires a teacher to critically analyze the work of these students and demonstrate how he or she can assist students who have different needs in their learning. These entries also document that the teacher continually assesses his or her learning and that of the students, and that from this assessment, classroom practice is modified.

The teachers who have engaged in this certification process generally feel that the first portfolio attempted is the most difficult. Jeannine Paszek

Figure 3.5

A Documented Accomplishment Entry

Reading Club

Under the professional entries, I've submitted documentation supporting my involvement with an after-school Reading Club. I've chosen to include two examples. The first is a verification form from my former principal acknowledging my participation, as well as summarizing exactly what the Reading Club was. The second document is an agenda from one of the meetings. I chose to highlight this activity because I believe it represents my efforts to establish open communication between parents and our community, the opportunity to develop an understanding of the principles and pedagogy of reading instruction, the opportunity to create a collaboration between parents and our school community, and finally the opportunity to offer understanding and strength for a stronger reading program for our children.

Candidate Name: *Barbara H. Surritte*

Below, briefly describe the accomplishment(s) being verified by the signer of the form. Explain **what** the accomplishment is and **why** it is noteworthy.

To continue to build the bridge between goals established by my state to increase reading scores and the community, I agreed to participate as a co-host of a Reading Club. The Reading Club would meet once a month in the evening. When we met, we would outline several different ways parents could become involved with their child's education, specifically, reading. Together with my partner, we outlined our school's objectives for teaching reading and reasons for those objectives. We completed exercises to facilitate reading at home and reviewed several different resources easily acquired to develop good learning habits, study skills, completion of homework and reading on a consistent basis. I feel that this accomplishment is noteworthy because by building a communication bridge between families and school, we are establishing a knowledge base of school expectations and goals, while the parents offer insights to their child's learning strengths and weakness, along with supporting the academic environment in which their child will be learning.

Is the candidate's description of his or her activities accurate?

___X___ Yes   _____ No   _____ Don't Know

How do you know of these activities?

I have first hand knowledge.
I had the pleasure of being Barbara Surritte's supervisor as the Principal at Silver Lake School. Barbara's club was always well-attended. Parents would stop me in the grocery store to tell me how much they enjoyed Reading Club. I feel the clubs contributed substantially to positive school-community relations as well as increasing parents knowledge and participation in their children's education.

Figure 3.5 *(continued)*

March Intermediate Reading Club
Welcome!

Reading Club Agenda
1. Entrance Activity:　Graph—What do you like to read?
　　　　　　　　　　　Make a personal nametag.
　　　　　　　　　　　Get a snack—Root beer floats!
2. Introductions and Mixer Activity:　People Search
3. Reading Strategy:　Reading—It's All Around Us!
4. Activities:　Poetry
　　　　　　　Poetry Treasure Hunt
　　　　　　　Poetry in Music
　　　　　　　Poetry in Magazines
　　　　　　　Write a Poem
5. Activities:　The Newspaper
　　　　　　　Newspaper Scavenger Hunt
　　　　　　　Reading the Newspaper
　　　　　　　Creative Writing—Newspaper Headlines
6. Closure:　Reading a Book

---

stated that "after completing the first portfolio entry, I had a much clearer idea of what was required."

After the first entry was completed, each teacher developed a method of attack for the following ones. For example, Jeanine VanDeVort, describes her method:

> As I took out each portfolio entry, I mentally organized my life for the next few months. Some entries required seeing how you organize a unit from beginning to end over a period of time. Student artifacts and written accounts of the unit's progression and students' progress over a four- to six-week period. The first portfolio I decided to tackle was language arts. Picking the two students whose work that I was going to use and submit as examples was not easy. All my students wanted me to pick their work. Deciding on a body of work I was going to showcase was agonizing. I finally decided to showcase a social studies project for which my students write an ending to the myth Atalanta.

Figure 3.6

Bloom's Taxonomy
Levels of Thinking

Classification	Question Cues	Student Activity
6 Evaluation	(Judging) Can you set standards, rate, select, and choose, decide, weigh according to; how do you feel about	Criticize, justify choices and actions, decide according to standard, prove
5 Synthesis	(Creating, adapting) Think of all the different ways, how else, can you design, improve, develop	Imagine, predict, design, improve, change, create, invent, adapt
4 Analysis	(Seeing parts of) How can you; what are the causes, consequences, steps of the process; can you arrange, examine	Compare, take apart, analyze, solve, contrast, dissect, investigate, discuss
3 Application	(Using, Solving problems) Can you use the information, demonstrate; can you solve	Apply, model, order, use acquired data in new learning situations, operate
2 Comprehension	(Showing that you understand) Can you tell in your own words, interpret, explain; what are the relationships	Classify, demonstrate, group, illustrate, rearrange, reorder
1 Knowledge	(Finding out) Can you tell, list, describe; do you remember; relate who, when, where, which, what; define	Memorize, gather data, name, observe, show, record, locate

Bloom, B., M. Engelhart, E. Gurst, W. Hill, and D. Krathwohl. 1984. *Taxonomy of Educational Objectives, Book 1: Cognitive Domains.* Boston: Allyn & Bacon.

A recommendation from this group of teachers and others is to scrutinize each portfolio entry and its expectations. Make a list of exactly what has to be done. Each entry is explicit with its unique requirements. After this evaluation of the expectations of each entry, a teacher will be better able to plan teaching units, as well as how and when snapshots for the National Board assessment process will be selected.

To make this process more explicit, see the samples of student work that were used by three teachers (Figure 3.7 and Appendix A). These examples should give you a clearer picture of how student work might be selected. Jeanine VanDeVort's work with the Atalanta myth is from her

Figure 3.7

Student Sample

Teaching across the curriculum is so important because it shows students how English, science, reading, math, and social studies are all connected. I want my students to realize that what they learn in one content area needs to be reinforced and developed in other content areas. Christina did an excellent job in transferring what she had learned in English to her social studies myth ending. I chose her work to demonstrate what what I valued about integration of content was actualized in the classroom.
From Jeanine VanDeVort

Christina's Myth
Just before Atalanta and Melanion started the race, Melanion ate a golden apple. He was sure that the magic powers of the apple would help him win the race.

Soon they began the race, Melanion was ahead of Atalanta. "The golden apple gave me speed," thought Melanion to himself.

Atalanta began to catch up to Melanion. He had stopped to catch his breath. While he was catching his breath, he had eaten the second golden apple. "The golden apple will give me even more speed and breath to last the whole race," he assured himself.

When he finally began to catch up to Atalanta again, his feet began to hurt. He stopped and ate the last golden apple. "My feet will feel much better," he said confidently to himself.

He at last caught up to Atalanta. Then a big surprise came to Melanion, Atalanta was talking to him. Melanion began to talk back. They both decided to run across the finish line together.

The next day they got married on the grassy fields where they ran the day before. Atalanta picked this place because it was special to her.

Her father was very proud and happy. He now had a son, but not only a son, a hero.

---

intermediate classroom. Before presenting the myth written by a student, Jeanine explains why this work was valued (see Figure 3.7). Carol Hines, a middle school teacher, shares the work she selected, which centered on a mini-unit on slavery and in particular on the Orphan Train (see Appendix A). In her sample, the connections from history to today are evident. The last sample comes from Jeannine Paszek, a high school science teacher, who shares her responses to a student's work and other related work (see Appendix A).

These three entries require the majority of time and effort from teachers engaged in this process. They have the greatest value, as demonstrated by the weights attached to them. And they require extensive planning, analysis, and reflection by a teacher. As you work through these entries, pay close attention to the section "Making Good Choices." This section provides guidance about each entry's requirements. Moreover, consider the section "How Will Your Response Be Scored?", which explains exactly what the scorers will be looking for. We found it helpful to give each completed entry a close read matched to this section. If something was missing, a teacher could go back and revise, knowing specifically what was needed.

Videotaping

Videotaping teaching seemed to be the part of the process that stressed the teachers the most. There were several considerations for videotaping. The first was making sure that the equipment worked and that microphones were placed so that all students could be heard. Some teachers used an overhead microphone because their rooms were small and this microphone picked up all discussion. Other teachers had a microphone that they moved from small group to small group as a group was featured on the video. In many circumstances, the teacher also wore a microphone. The assessment materials contain more suggestions for videotaping.

Jeannine Paszek talked about the specifics of videotaping in her room. She offers the following thoughts that you might consider as you think about videotaping:

> I selected a senior student who was responsible and competent to video in my classroom. I have a small classroom, with a carpeted floor, so we used a camera that has a directional microphone attached.

Basically, when the camera zooms in on a student who is speaking, the microphone zooms with it. I kept the students in their groups of four, but oriented them in a circle around the exterior of the room, with the video camera at the back of the room, leaving enough space to view all the students.

Beyond the sound issues, teachers need to consider the quality of the video. We ran into several problems here. One teacher had to move his students in the room so that he was not videotaping with a large window behind them. Although he did not like the new configuration, it supported getting a quality video. Another teacher videotaped a lesson that used computer-projected slides and experiments. Because his room was dark, it was hard to see the projected materials and the students. He spent time working on how to capture the work and students on the video. Each of these teachers discovered these problems by taking the opportunity to video early in the process. They were able to reconcile the problems so they did not interfere with teaching or obtaining a satisfactory video. If they had waited until the last minute, clearly, these glitches would not have had such a positive resolution.

In addition to the equipment and room configuration, a teacher needs to think about who will do the videotaping. The teachers used various people for this job. Some of the teachers used students, and that worked fine. Other teachers used teachers or student teachers. A few teachers used husbands or wives. And in one school, there was a program for students to become expert with media, and these students were recruited. The teachers found it important to prepare the videographer so that he or she would focus on the instruction they were trying to capture. If the video requirements were for large-group instruction, they wanted to capture themselves as they taught and the students' engagement. If the expectation was for small-group instruction with the teacher as a facilitator, it was important to capture the groups working with and without the teacher.

Barbara Surritte shares how she prepared the person who was videotaping in her room:

I actually took the guidelines from the entry and provided a copy for the videographer. We reviewed exactly what was required for the entry. We also set up the microphones on the floor and in two locations to cover the center-work taking place.

Finally, the teachers felt that they needed to video often, so that their students did not misbehave or freeze in front of the camera.

Jeannine Paszek, a high school science teacher, shares her thinking about one videotaping session. Her words might make it easier for you to reflect on how you will complete the videotaping expectations.

> This videotape needed to demonstrate how whole-class discussions about major science concepts are used as an integral part of an effective teacher's repertoire. The class I chose to videotape had a highly diverse population, in both their exterior appearance and their insights. I wrote my questions on index cards the night before, and felt ready to roll the tape. I stood in front of the class, unencumbered by a desk or podium, so that I would feel free to roam the room when I gave students time to brainstorm ideas.
>
> Time seemed to fly by while the discussion was taking place. The directed questions that I had created incorporated current events that led students to make connections between the real world and the science concept, as well as evoking an emotional response that would make for a more passionate discussion. This allowed students to take leadership roles during the course of the discussion, which created a situation where students were dominating the discussion—exactly what I had hoped for. And with my cards in hand, I could bring the discussion back toward my goal. Also, implementing active learner strategies ensured inclusion of all students in the whole-group discussion.
>
> As far as I knew, the discussion had been a success and I was anxious to find out if the tape turned out—had video and sound! I went to watch the tape and was relieved to find that I could hear and see the tape!
>
> That weekend I spent almost an entire day writing the script from the tape. I wanted to include verbatim the things the students had said during the course of the discussion. I made a visual-characteristic seating chart (i.e., the girl in the red sweater rather than a student's name) and a script from the discussion. I used this information in the commentary about the videotape.

Jeannine's description includes the specifics of how she prepared for this event. She also shares how she transcribed the words of the students to include in her commentary. Several candidates did this scripting so that they could personalize their commentaries and include the voices of students in their write-ups.

In addition to the positive experiences during videotaping, there were many negative events, as might be expected. One teacher discovered that she had forgotten to put in a tape and had to teach the lesson again. Several teachers had children who froze when they were first videotaped; they had to talk to the students and do it again. Another teacher had to stop videotaping because of a fire drill. Because the tapes have time constraints and cannot be edited, she had to begin again. And one teacher was working with his students in a science lab when the school police entered to arrest one of his students. Amazingly, his students never stopped working on their labs. They ignored the whole event. Because the lesson was so powerful in itself and the students continued working through the arrest, he decided to include it in his entry. There was no problem with confidentiality because only feet of the student and police were captured on the video. This teacher is now a National Board teacher.

Remember, to reduce anxiety, it is best to start videotaping early and videotape often in the process. Students and you need to stop focusing on the camera and focus on the teaching and learning. The National Board is not looking for professional videos; the scorers want videos that demonstrate accomplished teaching.

Finally, here are a few suggestions that helped with the videotape results. Use high-quality videotapes, and remember that the part you want to use will be copied. The video entries all have specific time limits and they cannot be edited. The scorer will assess only the part of the tape that fits the time limit. So, if your tape runs twenty-five minutes and the expectation was for a fifteen-minute video, the scorer will watch only the first fifteen minutes. This assures each candidate that he or she is being treated fairly.

Beyond time, think about the clothes that you will wear. Wear simple, comfortable clothes so that you do not squirm and fiddle with them during the taping. Rehearse your lesson so that you are not worrying about what might happen next. For these lessons, you need to be prepared ahead of time. This preparation should facilitate a well-done video that satisfies the criteria.

Writing

Each teacher is expected to complete a written commentary for each entry. These commentaries complement the videos or student work samples.

Our cohort compared them and the artifacts to a picture book. In a picture book the illustrations and text support each another. A picture book is successful when the illustrations and the text enhance and enrich each other; otherwise, the story is not complete. This analogy holds up for the National Board entries as well. The written commentaries are expected to fill in what might not be explicit in the video or student sample. When the commentary is coupled with the video or student work, a whole story is told; one part complements the other.

The National Board expects a teacher to use descriptive, analytical, and reflective writing for these commentaries. The National Board has defined each type of writing. The definitions follow.

- *Descriptive writing*—a retelling of a lesson, or a description of students and the activity. For this type of writing a teacher needs to provide a clear and accurate description that includes supporting details or examples. When a teacher is sharing a lesson or activity, it should be ordered logically so that a reader gains the important features of it. This writing provides the grounding for analytical and reflective writing.

- *Analytical writing*—an explanation of the reasons behind the choices that were made by the teacher. The teacher would explain why a lesson was structured the way it was or why a student's work was selected with an analysis of the work. The goal of this writing is to explain why. And the teacher is encouraged to always go back to the standards and the requirements of the entry to make sure that his or her analysis ties to these explicit expectations.

- *Reflective writing*—a self-analysis of a teacher's practice and analysis of student learning. Here the teacher looks back at a lesson and considers how the lesson might be revised to enhance student learning.

Carol Hines helped all the candidates in our cohort with their writing by compiling a list of words that could be used to meet these writing expectations. She grouped words by type of writing, and this may help you as well (see Figure 3.8).

Perhaps the best advice about writing is, answer the questions posed. Jessica Daniels provides this advice to other candidates when she says, "You don't need to be cute, clever, or creative, but you must *answer the question that is asked*."

Figure 3.8

Helpful Vocabulary to Use in Writing Entries

Carol Hines developed this list to help find the perfect word for an entry.

Analyze

Appreciate	Compare	Establish	Inventory	Share
Arrange	Comprehend	Examine	Investigate	Study
Assess	Consider	Experiment	Know	Survey
Assist	Coordinate	Explore	Learn	Talk about
Be acquainted	Detect	Find out	Maintain	Test
with	Diagram	Grasp significance	Monitor	Think about
Be aware of	Differentiate	of	Organize	Understand
Be interested in	Discover	Group	Prioritize	Value
Believe	Discuss	Have insight into	Prove	
Categorize	Dissect	Inquire	Realize	
Classify	Distinguish	Inspect	Recognize	
Communicate	Engage	Interpret	Scrutinize	

Extend Understandings

Assemble	Design	Hypothesize	Predict	Suppose
Compose	Develop	Imagine	Prepare	Systematize
Concoct	Devise	Incorporate	Pretend	Theorize
Construct	Forecast	Invent	Project	
Contrive	Formulate	Originate	Set up	
Create	Generalize	Plan	Speculate	

Describe

Adapt	Construct	Exhibit	Name	Revise
Adjust	Contrast	Expand	Operate	Role-play
Alter	Convert	Explain	Organize	Select
Analyze	Correct	Find	Outline	Sort
Apply	Create	Formulate	Participate	Speak
Arrange	Define	Gather	Perform	Specify
Assemble	Demonstrate	Generate	Plan	State
Build	Describe	Identify	Plot	Summarize
Calculate	Design	Interpret	Prepare	Teach
Categorize	Determine	Justify	Present	Trace
Choose	Develop	List	Read	Use
Cite	Display	Listen	Record	Utilize
Classify	Estimate	Locate	Research	Weigh
Collect	Evaluate	Match	Respond	Write
Compare	Examine	Measure	Review	

All the teachers struggled with this part of the process. We vacillated between including the questions that must be answered in our writing to writing in the form of an essay. Just answering the questions bothered some of the teachers who were experienced writers. They did not like the breaks in the text because they interrupted the flow. In the end, the decision was to write the questions in the text and provide the answers directly after them. If a teacher ran out of room (remember the page limits), the questions were removed from the final draft. However, having a question in preliminary drafts helped the teachers know if they had answered a question completely.

Beyond directly answering the questions, the teachers included in the text the standards that were being addressed. When a teacher's practice met a standard, he or she put the standard in parentheses near the description or analysis. In this way, a teacher could reread an entry and be convinced that the necessary standards were achieved. He or she could also tell if one standard was predominant and a better balance might need to be achieved. As with the questions, if there was not room for the standards in the final draft, they were cut after the teacher knew they were clearly addressed.

All the teachers found readers who would respond critically to their written commentaries. The readers were given the standards that were required to be met and information about how the entry would be scored. Readers used these documents to provide the necessary feedback to each candidate. Once the critical aspects of the entry were addressed, the reader offered micro-editing comments. The National Board does not deduct points for errors in spelling, grammar, or punctuation, but the teachers wanted their entries to be as clean as possible. They did not want a scorer to be distracted from the content of their entry by minor mistakes.

The Assessment Center

The assessment center exercises now require teachers to answer six, thirty-minute prompts centered on content knowledge. In the past, teachers participated in this portion of the assessment after they had completed their portfolio. Now the timing of the assessment center is varied. Teachers request their half-days in January; their scheduled date for these exercises may be before or after their portfolio is sent. Teachers who are scheduled to visit the assessment center prior to sending their portfolios will need to revise their schedules. They may need to take some time from their portfolio entries to make sure they are confident of the content related to their discipline. For generalists, this content is quite broad. For content area specialists, the content is narrowed to one area or discipline; however, teachers are expected to know more than just the content they teach. So a biology teacher would need to know about general science, chemistry, physics, and so on, in addition to the chosen focus area. Teachers often pick the content they are most knowledgeable about as their focus area. Jeannine Paszek shares how she made this decision:

> To make this decision, I looked toward my teaching assignment for the upcoming school year; it included regular chemistry. First, I decided it would be a wise investment of my time to review my college-level general chemistry in preparation. Second, I still had confidence in my biology background, and I had just recently completed a general physics course. Third, I incorporated many earth science concepts into my general science program, so I felt that these concepts were still fresh in my mind. So after weighing all my assets, I selected chemistry as my area of focus.

Jeannine selected chemistry to focus her assessment center questions; another teacher might have considered the same issues and come away with a different area of focus. This is another decision that is very important to teachers in some disciplines. In other areas, such as early childhood, no such choices are offered.

Teachers receive material that prepares them for the assessment center exercises. The application book and the National Board's web site detail areas that will be assessed to prepare teachers for this part of the process as well. Although in the past teachers have been able to bring materials to the test site, this is no longer appropriate. Teachers can bring only identification materials to the site; no support material is allowed.

This part of the assessment process places incredible stress on the teachers. They always have numerous questions pertaining to it. One thing to remember is that this portion of the assessment is about 40 percent of the whole assessment process. The scores that you receive on these exercises are not weighted as much as those on the portfolio entries.

Other details for teachers involve the computers and word-processing skills necessary to complete these exercises. Most teachers use the computers. Currently teachers can elect to handwrite their responses, but this option is not expected to be available much longer. Of course, there are exceptions. In science and math, portions of answers require handwriting to complete (e.g., creating tables or solving problems with formulas). Additionally, teachers of languages other than English have to handwrite a part of this assessment because the computers are not equipped to generate all the necessary diacritical marks.

On a computer, when the question or prompt is posed to a teacher, he or she will often see a split screen. The question may be on one part of the computer screen while next to it may be some information needed to answer the question. At the bottom of the screen will be a place for the teacher to compose his or her answer. This format helps teachers with each question because they do not have to scroll up or down the screen to refer to information needed for the response.

Teachers need to remember that at the end of the allotted time (thirty minutes), they will no longer be able to work on a particular response. It will be submitted and they will be encouraged to move on to the next prompt. Teachers may take breaks between exercises. To practice these exercises, a candidate can go the National Board's web site and sign in to the candidate support area, where practice exercises are available. This practice is very beneficial; it allows you to go through a simulation of an exercise and get familiar with the prompts and time constraints.

As you might imagine, the teachers who contributed to this chapter had a lot to say about the assessment center. All the teachers were stressed about this part of the assessment. I chose to share Cora Carrigan's words because her situation was unique: The attendant at the assessment center could not locate her name and she was delayed in beginning her assessment. She relates:

> I drove to the center with my handwritten materials and the forms for identification. I met Ginny (another teacher) and three other members of our cohort. We were all nervous and anxious to get started and gradually they began calling people in, one at a time. The clock continued ticking and one hour later, things came to a standstill. Ginny and I were the remaining two people. The director informed us that they were having difficulty calling up our programs because they were new certification areas. Ginny and I kept telling each other to be calm. We sat and quietly shredded the leaves on the fake plant between us.

After another forty-five minutes, the director returned and said that he had our programs ready.

Although it was incredibly frustrating for Cora and Ginny to wait, they had support from each other. As they found, one way to reduce stress at the center is to schedule the same time with a friend. In this way, the teachers can take breaks together and relax and support each other through the exercises.

As we have reflected on the whole process, we have rethought the assessment center quite a bit. Certainly, teachers need to go to the center confident in their knowledge of the content they teach. They need to be ready for unforeseen problems at the center, like those experienced by Cora and Ginny. Moreover, we think that each teacher should have someone with whom to debrief after the assessment center. Many of the teachers felt quite lonely going home after this labor-intensive session. They wanted to share or vent about it. In the future, we plan to structure a debriefing time for candidates who want it. In this way, there will be someone to recognize the tremendous effort put forth by each teacher.

The Long Wait

This part of the process requires extreme patience. For most teachers, the entire assessment process is completed by early summer. Then they must wait until the end of November or beginning of December to hear the results. Many teachers grew tired of friends and colleagues asking if they knew yet. Moreover, each teacher took a great risk when he or she entered this process. While everyone understood that this rigorous process had a less that 50 percent pass rate for the first attempt, this knowledge began to prey on them. The teachers became more focused on passing or not passing by early fall. They expressed concern about how they would handle not being successful on their first attempt. How would they share this news with colleagues, friends, and family? Other teachers worried about how the cohort would handle the results when not every teacher was successful. Jessica Daniels describes her feelings during this time:

When results time draws near, just the sight of the NBPTS logo may be enough to send your heart reeling and a tidal wave of nausea plummeting to the pit of your stomach. This could leave you vulnerable to the following ailments:

1. Panic attacks: Please be advised the letter with the NBPTS logo that may arrive at school the same week scores are announced will not need to be hidden on your desk. It is, I emphasize, not your results. It is most likely a letter of encouragement.

2. You might also suffer a severe bout of "I'm chicken to look at the web–itis." This can leave you delusional while you wait for the NBPTS envelope. If the media folk call, they have probably been to the web site and they know something that you should know. So go visit the web.

The National Board has outlined a process for teachers to be informed of their results. During the first years of the process, each candidate received a letter with the news before the results were posted to the National Board's web site. This past year, the teachers learned about passing or not passing when their names were posted on the web site. This was the first time many teachers learned their results. Many were frustrated when they could not gain access to the web site to discover their personal results and others informed them. For example, Cora learned of her success from her daughter in Washington, D.C. She describes the event this way:

> I was teaching when I received two nearly simultaneous phone calls, one from my daughter who announced, "Mom your name is on it . . . you passed." I had a classroom full of kids and I burst into tears. We hung up and the phone rang again. It was Ginny and she congratulated me and said that both she and her daughter had passed.

Jeanine VanDeVort learned that she was successful when there was an announcement over the intercom that she had passed.

Other teachers discovered that they were not successful on their first attempt. For Petrina McCarty-Puhl, this news was difficult to hear, as it would be for any teacher. She was able to get to the web site, but her name was not there. Later she found that there were some mistakes on the web site and hoped that her name's not being there was one of them. A few days later the envelope from the National Board arrived and she discovered that she had missed certifying by only one point. Her composure left her at this point.

I recalculated the scores and found that if I had just received one-fourth of a point more I would have passed once the weight had been applied. I threw the calculator across the room. I stormed! I yelled! I have never been more frustrated in my life.

When Margaret Thiel discovered that she had not passed, her reaction was quite different from that of Petrina. She arrived home and her husband was there with the news that he could not find her name on the web site. Her reaction was to "cry big tears." Her husband held her until she could get hold of her emotions. Margaret had risked this process in a small community of people who were all supportive of her throughout the process. As the members of her community commiserated with her, she constantly broke down in tears. Eventually her son said to her, "Mom, no one died, you can fix this." With his words she realized that she was still a qualified teacher and she determined to continue the process until she was successful.

The National Board was concerned with the way teachers were notified of their results this past year. In the future, teachers will be sent a letter and there will be approximately four days when only candidates will have access to the web site results. The dates when the site is open to candidates will be posted on the National Board's web site in November. In this way, each candidate can learn of his or her results before the news becomes public.

After the results are announced, each teacher needs time to work through his or her emotions. In our cohort, when everyone's emotions settled down, the work began again. The teachers who were successful were willing to support those who needed another year. The teachers who missed certification banked their scores and reentered the process. They are retaking a few entries to improve their scores. These scores, whether higher or lower, will be combined with their previous scores. They are currently waiting to learn the results of their retakes and their final scores.

Teachers have two years to retake entries. When they receive their scores, teachers can choose to retake entries that they scored low on. The entries are marked that can be retaken on the results sheet. Teachers need to consider their scores and the weighting of scores as they plan which entries to retake. Remember, the new score will replace the old score whether it is higher or lower. A candidate cannot select the higher score. Candidates are sent information about this retake process so that they can engage in it thoughtfully.

Final Thoughts

Each teacher in our cohort discovered the reasons for his or her successes with students. They all thought that this was the most effective professional development of their lives. They learned how to make their teaching even more effective through the analysis and reflection that is the core of this process. While it was difficult and a constant challenge, they welcomed the new insights about their teaching and students' learning that resulted.

Following the process, the National Board Certified Teachers are providing leadership in their schools and the community. Many are working with new candidates and others are providing professional development to colleagues in other ways. Most important, they are all continuing to provide exemplary teaching to students. They are able to provide professional support to others as they simultaneously teach to the highest standards. The students who are fortunate to be in their classrooms will benefit from the teaching of these teachers, enjoying learning and exhibiting deeper understanding of the subjects taught to them.

Freshwater Fish in a Saltwater Pond

Leo McBride

It was already late in the year, perhaps September, when I heard of a meeting for teachers in our school district interested in achieving National Board Certification. I had no idea what was involved in doing this, but I thought the incentive was attractive: a small raise in pay and no state recertification for ten years; plus, some national mobility should I need that or desire to relocate. Since my wife was pursuing her advanced degree, and she had followed me to this state for my current job, I thought it only fair that I be ready and able to follow her if that became our best option. I had also heard that people who had done it felt it was very good professional development, perhaps the best thing they had done for their teaching in their entire career. Sounded like some great rewards!

The orientation meeting was very informative, but I left it undecided as to whether to pursue the National Board for Professional Teaching Standards (NBPTS) certificate. My main concern was the same one I carried with me through the entire process, and that was the nagging question, "Does this really apply to my teaching area?" The certificate area I would have to apply for was English/Language Arts for high school students, but I am not an English teacher. I do have a degree in English with an emphasis in writing, but I teach drama and theater arts. I have a master's degree in theater. I taught English my first year, and drama exclusively ever since—ten years. For the last five years I have been teaching in an upper middle-class high school, with a full-time drama program. I direct three plays per year; every other year a full-scale musical is part of that schedule. I am a busy man, but the time commitment sounded to me like something I could handle in a nonmusical year.

The fact remained that I still was unsure about the appropriateness of my area, theater, in the English/Language Arts certificate area. The facilitator at the meeting kept saying I would certainly qualify under that category, and that there was a drama teacher in another part of the state who was also pursuing the certificate. I left the meeting thinking I wanted to do it, but doubting that I could stretch what I do far enough to make it work for what seemed to be an area mainly for English teachers. There simply was no sample of the kinds of entries I would have to make for the portfolio. If I had those available, I most likely would have decided to wait for something more appropriate for my area. As of this writing, I do not know if I passed.

I encourage you to look hard at the certificates and be sure you are teaching what they are assessing. That doubt in my mind made the process the most stressful thing I have done in my life, except living through double bypass heart surgery!

Interruptions, Interruptions

They say that you should do this in a year when your personal life is and will likely remain fairly calm. Do not do it if you expect to have a baby, get a divorce or get married, have an illness or disease that periodically stops your work routines, or have sick or dying relatives who will take away your focus. My life was stable, as it was for most people in our cohort, until I paid the money and got the materials. NBPTS pursuits seemed to have a way of destroying a lot of that for a lot of us.

A death in my family in late September threw things off early. Then my brother-in-law decided to get married in April, and wanted my wife and me to sing at the wedding, which was, of course, 1,800 miles away. Then my sister needed to have her kidney removed and of course all the family would gather around to support her in that, again out of town. Such situations happened to others in our group. A colleague broke her foot, had taken into her home the foreign exchange student from hell, her husband was involved in a car crash in which his injuries led doctors to discover that he had cancer, and she herself had been periodically seriously ill for about three years. Another colleague's husband seemed anything but supportive, and she had all kinds of problems with students that year. I suppose the moral of this story is, you can't control what will happen, but if you take on the National Board, be prepared for life to get worse!

Support Group

After I made the decision to go for it, I felt confident that I could indeed do this. Our facilitator was the key in that confidence (along with my wife, also a teacher). She scheduled regular meetings at which we could discuss how the process was going for each of us. We could commiserate with others in our certificate area and share knowledge and experience, critique entries, watch each other's videos, and generally help one another through this process. If not for those meetings and the encouragement of the others in the cohort, I would never have completed the portfolio. Because of them I didn't feel all alone, which turned out to be extremely important. On a day when I would feel like I wasn't doing anything right regarding the NBPTS, I'd walk in and listen to what others were doing and think, "I'm doing better than that," or "that's exactly what I did!" Thanks to all of them just for getting me to the point of submitting my work!

Roll Up Your Sleeves and Dig In

Now, for the work itself. The entries were set up so that one could choose any order in which to work on them. I decided that because of my schedule at school, with a play going on just then, I should wait until December to actually begin. Big mistake!

In December, during winter vacation, I thought I would work on the NBPTS through much of the two weeks and get a lot done. That was when I faced a major crisis. As I really began to delve into it, the doubt in my mind about my area fitting the category grew to mammoth proportions. I thought I would have to stretch things so far to make it look like I was fitting the category in my classroom that I would receive a telegram from the people scoring my entries reading, "What are you trying to pull?" It totally stopped me for two days, and took an entire daylong discussion with my wife to convince me I should continue to work on the entries. We talked, we laughed, we cried, we yelled, and we made up, and then did it all some more. She made me realize that in one way or another I already do in my classroom all the things they were asking for. She showed me that I was doing much more than teaching drama. I was really teaching language arts and doing "English" kinds of things in my drama classroom. I just didn't recognize it as such. Finally, by nightfall, I was a candidate again. I was not without that doubt, but at least it had diminished.

I should have begun right away to gather the evidence I needed for the Professional Development and Parent Involvement entries, to get the verifications and permissions and all the little details done first. That, unfortunately, is not my style. I am a procrastinator, and for my fellow procrastinators reading this, to get this done you will need an incredible last-minute surge such as you've never had in your life. Best advice—put off your putting off! To sort of ease into it, force yourself to spend one hour every day working on the little things first, such as the photocopying of the driver's license and the information gathering that is required for your school's data, and so forth. Then increase that each week to a manageable amount of time in order to balance all of life's demands.

Spend a good amount of time thinking about which class you will use for each entry and which students you will use as your samples. Plan how you will do the videos, get the equipment together, and practice recording. You may find out you talk a lot more than your students do, and you may need to break that pattern for certain types of entries. Watching yourself on camera may be painful at first. You are bound to be critical of yourself, your style, your clothing, your weight, or your gray hair. You may also find that the setup of your room needs adjustment to obtain a high-quality recording of your lesson. Trial tapes will get you past all that, so you will be all business when you do it for real. Plan your units according to your NBPTS plan, and then start with whichever one you think will be the easiest to accomplish; that will give you a boost of confidence right away.

When I did begin, I started with the small-group discussion because I thought I could answer the first part of the entry's questions fairly easily, which I did. Then before shooting the video, I went on to work on the Professional Development entry and the Parents and Families entry. Those were pretty successful for me, which made me feel better. I felt as if I had at least gotten some of it behind me, and was really going to do this thing! That had a great effect on my confidence. I still hadn't gathered all my evidence, but at least the writing of those two entries was mostly done.

By February, I had two entries mostly written, and two others started. The next thing was gathering student release forms and continuing to gather evidence. I chose one of those days when extracurricular activities are going on in the building and any attempt to do *real* classroom work seemed futile. I was able to discuss the NBPTS process fully with my students and answer their questions about it, and to show them how important it was to me and how much I needed their help. This gave them some ownership in my process. Last year's students still ask me about the outcome of it all.

I shot one video of the small-group discussion, watched it that night, and reshot the next day. That was it for the first video. I felt that I had done a fair job on the second day, and that the assignment I had selected was the only one I could use that particular class for. It was a timing issue, I suppose, as much as anything else. I honestly felt that representation of my teaching and my students' learning was as good as it would get.

The second video took more preparation because it was the whole-class discussion, and I had to wait for the unit I had chosen to roll around. I had to prepare a set of questions to stimulate and direct the discussion in the way I thought would elicit a lot of conversation. I was on a major evaluation year at school, which meant that I had to demonstrate a specific level of proficiency in an area that I had identified as one in which I wanted to improve. It was while taping that second video, during the whole-class discussion, that my principal decided to observe me! No pressure, right? It turned out fine, and maybe his presence in class that day made me crank it up a notch. Maybe.

From doing the videos, I learned that when I took the time to instruct my students specifically on what I expected from them during the videotaping process, they responded appropriately. I told them that I wanted them to be involved in the discussion and if they weren't interested in doing that, to *act* as if they were. I told them to pretend they were on television discussing a play, and that their perceived knowledge and intellect may just get them a part in a new blockbuster movie that would make them a star. I told them I expected the behavior of young ladies and gentlemen. Of course, they're actors. In all areas, they came through. The principal was impressed and my evaluation was excellent.

The other two entries, which involved selecting students, were the hardest for me. The writing and reading presented the *stretch* for me as a teacher of drama rather than English. Of course we do read in drama, and we do occasionally write, but not geared toward the same goals as in an English class. I agonized for weeks over what to do to get the kind of sample they were expecting in the entry and at the same time not compromise my students by doing something that was just for my National Board process. These two entries held me up from completing the portfolio when I anticipated.

It was now mid-March, and I still had four entries to finish writing, two to polish, and verification and evidence to gather. I had not yet copied the videos to their allotted twenty minutes and had done nothing as far as looking at how to send this all in to the NBPTS. Plus, I was in the late stages of our second production of the year with one more to do. We had to rehearse our songs for my brother-in-law's wedding and my sister's surgery was approaching. I could feel the ceiling slowly moving down harder on my head as the walls were crushing me on all sides.

The Bottom of the Ninth

I took three days off from school to finish things up. Our teacher's association had negotiated three days of professional leave specifically for NBPTS candidates working on the process. During these three days things really fell into place. This was when I did most of the writing on the entries that involved my analysis of students and of my teaching. I had a quiet house and no interruptions, so I was able to think clearly. I wasn't rushed or worried, and I felt comfortable.

I didn't finish by my goal date, but I felt that I would finish. We left for the wedding and I planned that upon return I could begin finalizing and packing. When we came back we had only three days in town before we had to leave for my sister's surgery. It was a four-hour drive, and we would leave on a Friday morning about 6:00 A.M.

The night before leaving, I decided I was ready to pack my assessment materials. I began printing out all my finished entries, organizing, labeling, and coordinating, which I thought would take about four hours. I started about 5:00 P.M. I found I needed to make some copies of my entries, and of my evidence and student papers, so I went to school about 10:00 P.M. Thursday. It took much longer to make the copies than I anticipated. I also did some labeling of the entries with all the little stickers that the NBPTS supplied. I came back home about 1:00 A.M. Friday, and then copied my two videos.

At 5:00 A.M. Friday when my wife woke up to get ready for the trip, I was still up. I was in deep despair. One of the envelopes in The Box was missing. I had enough envelopes, but one was incorrectly labeled. I figured that was my punishment for not having checked them closely when I got them in November. I now felt that particular entry would be rejected because of this glitch. The instructions had said it was my responsibility to be sure all would be well upon opening The Box. I had heard other candidates had waited for weeks to get correct envelopes from the NBPTS home office. I knew it was all over for me. It had not been meant to be from the start and I was a fool for ever having tried this.

We left for San Francisco at 6:00 A.M. and I took my Box with me. My sister's surgery was on Monday morning. From the hospital I called the NBPTS offices and talked with someone there who told me I could correct the label myself and it would be acceptable. Relief! I took her name and thanked her profusely. When we returned home I did the deed on the label, checked and rechecked everything forty times, then sealed it all up, took it to the post office, sent it by the fastest service possible, insured it for $2,000, and kissed it goodbye (literally)! The postal worker thought I was nuts. I was.

On the way home from the post office, I cried, nay, I sobbed. It was finally over! I was so happy. It had been so hard, so stressful, and so consuming that I declared I would never start something like this again. I decided then and there that if I failed two entries I would redo them, but if I failed any more than that, I was through.

No Rest for the Wicked

My wife reminded me that I still had to take the test at the assessment center. I was resolved to work on that part of it diligently as soon as the reading list arrived. I didn't. She did. She gathered a lot of information for me off the Internet, finding information on art, music, literature, even downloading some of the poetry I needed so I wouldn't have to scrounge around looking through books in other people's homes and garages. She found information on the Vietnam Memorial in Washington and on its designer.

She e-mailed people asking for any of the texts and videos they had from the list. She was determined to help me through this part of it.

When June arrived, so did out-of-town family. I read and studied night and day, missed out on fun stuff with family, and probably gained fifteen pounds. There was so much to read and now I thought it was ridiculous. Had I been an English teacher instead of a drama teacher, I would already know a lot of this, I kept telling myself. Again that doubt crept in. As the days grew short, I got tired of reading and thinking. I started to give up. I was sick of it all and wanted it to be over. I got angry, with myself for beginning this stupid thing, with my wife for pushing me, with my colleague for being an English teacher, and with the NBPTS for not having a certificate in my area so I could have been a success. I was whining big time.

Testing day arrived. I was up early and felt resolved. I was just going to do my best and take my chances. I had decided that I was a good drama teacher, and if I didn't pass, it didn't diminish that. I went in and took my test. It was as I had anticipated, all about teaching methods as an *English* teacher. I answered the questions as best I could, and left four hours later.

That night my wife and I went out for dinner with my English teacher colleague and her husband, now recovered from cancer. The foreign exchange student from hell was leaving in a few days. Things were getting better for all of us. We decided to go to a movie the next day, which we did. We went out for dinner again that evening and watched a video at their home that night. We talked about "boards" and the test, and the more we talked the more I felt as if I had done well on the test. A few days later my wife and I took off on a vacation to see family. All was normal again.

A Few Deep Breaths Later

As I await the notification from the NBPTS, I think back on it all and ask myself, "was it worth it?" If I pass, it was, of course, worth it. But for me, if I do not pass, I'm not sure that all I went through was worth it just as a professional development activity. If I do not pass, I will forever blame myself for not waiting for an appropriate certificate area. I will forever feel that I was a freshwater fish in a saltwater pond. If I do pass, I will have to start to believe what my wife has been telling me for years—that I am a very good teacher who does not realize how much I really do teach my students, even in a drama class. If that's how this turns out, it was more than worth it.

5

And Miles to Go Before I Sleep

Mandy Campbell

I was in my tenth year of teaching and felt confident and ready to share my skills. I had completed my master's degree in literacy six years earlier and had taken university classes as well as in-service classes since then. Nevertheless, without realizing it, I was in need of a new challenge. When a colleague said, "I'm thinking about doing this National Board thing. Are you at all interested?" I quickly answered, "Yes!" although I knew almost nothing about it. I figured being nationally certified meant you could teach in any state. Although I had no plans to move, I was still interested. I had read somewhere that National Board Certification would be a way to give merit pay to teachers. Eventually I learned there was a proposal to grant National Board Certified Teachers a 5 percent raise in my state of Nevada. Given all this, I was intrigued and wanted to learn more about it. What clarified the issue for me was when I learned that no one in the state of Nevada was certified; then I became very motivated and determined to be one of the first.

"What's the deal?" I asked, hoping, I suppose, to hear how easy National Board Certification would be. My colleague explained it was a yearlong process of self-evaluation that would require a lot of writing. "Cool. I love to write."

My master's thesis had been on the opening of my new high school, and I had enjoyed writing it. If the process for certification was anything like writing my thesis, I knew I had a lot of work ahead of me, but that it would be fun. My only hesitation was that I was getting married the following April, but I figured if I could finish the project before the wedding, I could do it. "When is it all due?" As it turned out, the portfolio part was due April 17, the week before my wedding; that was a sign for me to give it a shot. It's funny to think of it now because I had no idea of what I was getting into—marriage and the National Board all in one year.

I began communicating with Dr. Barone at the university who was going to facilitate the first Northern Nevada group through the process. The plan was she would set up monthly meetings for us to support each other. It all sounded doable. My husband-to-be, also a teacher, was very supportive and told me to "go for it" if that's what I wanted to do. He was coaching football and dealing with seniors in his government classes, so he was extremely busy, too.

Cost was another issue. The cost was $2,000 up front, but there was lots of talk of grants and scholarships, and then our teacher's association offered loans at 0 percent interest for National Board candidates. Who could ask for a better deal than that? I was one of the first teachers to receive this generous loan; it seemed to me everything was falling into place.

Four other teachers at my school were also considering tackling this new certification, so I knew I'd have a built-in support system. I felt that I was meant to go through this process at this time, and I was really excited to be doing something challenging and new.

Going Through the Certification Process

I went on-line several times (www.nbpts.org), learning all I could about the National Board for Professional Teaching Standards (NBPTS) and the certification process. I sent the money and anxiously awaited my materials. I read somewhere that the certification process would require something in the range of 300 to 400 hours. "Whatttttt?"

That amount of time seemed impossible. I got out my calculator and began running some numbers. If it would take 400 hours, and I had six or seven months to complete it, that's over 60 hours per month or 15 hours per week working on the project for the next seven months. "No way!" I was in a silent panic. It would be impossible for me to find 15 hours a week for twenty-eight weeks straight to work on anything other than teaching five English classes and trying to keep up on the grading and planning (oh, and planning a wedding and honeymoon!).

Those of us pursuing certification had our first group meeting in October. A couple of my group members had already received their boxes of materials from the NBPTS, and I was anxious to pore through them. Although they were seeking certification in different areas from me, going over the "Getting Started" specifics helped. We checked out what to do first, and how to break down the entire portfolio process into the six entries.

Six big papers in over six months? "I can do this!" What I really wanted to see was what the final outcome would look like. Then I would have a better idea of what I needed to do and how I could accomplish my goal. I'm rather systematic, you see. We never were able to see any portfolio entry in its entirety, which was frustrating. How was I to know how to make my entries excellent if I had no standard to go by? Later when we did get to see single-page excerpts of entries and I got a better sense of the standards expected via all the checklists and specifics provided, I felt more confident.

The Box

I received my NBPTS box for certification in Adolescent and Young Adult English/Language Arts on October 4 and began to get organized. The contents of The Box included the two-inch-thick portfolio binder of instructions along with every item needed to organize the portfolio for submission. Our first meeting's discussion—"the importance of clear videotaping," "good microphones," "save everything," "know the standards," "do your forms early," "get verifications," and so on—had been too abstract for me. I needed to sit down and read through my portfolio materials and get a picture of what the project would look like. I set up a schedule for myself based on the generic schedule provided in the introduction section of my materials. It listed:

Month 1:   Receive portfolio materials
           Read the "Step by Step" section, the "Standards" section, and all portfolio directions.

Month 2:　Begin to describe your accomplishments . . .
(NBPTS, AYAELA, Introduction, p.17).

I checked things off as I read through them: Receive portfolio materials
(✓), Read "Step by Step" section (✓), Read the "Standards" section (✓),
and so on.

I began breathing a little easier once I received my materials, but the
truth is I had to read each and every portfolio description and section several times to gain a sense of what was expected. I read and reread, and
wrote down questions, and underlined, and summarized each entry even
before I started doing the work. I had to understand what my goal was in
order to begin!

Getting Started

I think the best way to start on the portfolio is to get a general idea of all the
different entries by reading them. Then candidates should look at their
yearly curricular goals to make a plan for each entry. I wanted to start on my
classroom and videotaping entries; however, all of them required ongoing
work, which took several months to acquire. For example, one of my portfolio entries asked that I show student work from two students tackling
three units, and show their final projects from each. I had to organize my
required school district curricula to ensure I had good materials to include,
but I also had to teach at least three different units to reach this goal.

It seemed all the classroom entries required long-term materials, so all
I could do was plan ahead and save everything. "Save everything" is the
official mantra for the certification process, but I didn't know the importance of it until I was writing my entries near the end of the process. I
thought certain students would be good candidates for my entry explana-
tions, but I learned it was best to save several students' work to have it
available for consideration. I didn't know until all the student samples were
in front of me which combination of students and their work would be
best to write about in my entries. Since I always store students' major
papers for each semester anyway, I was able to look through all their folders to decide whose work to include.

The Documented Accomplishments entries are a good place to start
writing because they are the only entries candidates can work on before the

Figure 5.1

A Documented Accomplishment Entry

One of the expectations for National Board candidates is that they share professional accomplishments that have direct connections to student learning. Following is one teacher's choice of a professional accomplishment and the evidence to support this claim.

Reason for selection: This accomplishment demonstrates national involvement tied directly to teaching in the classroom. Students become aware that this teacher is working with others in professional ways. In addition, the students benefit by seeing what other students in the nation are doing, thus broadening their awareness of the expertise of other students.

```
A portion of the written commentary

… Additionally, for the past three years I have been a
judge for NCTE's Secondary Schools National Literary
Magazine Award Program [Document 4-B]. I receive 2 to 4
literary magazines to judge. I get to keep each magazine I
judge and enjoy sharing them with my students…

My work in these areas does impact students. I have shared
with my students that I am a reviewer and judge. This shows
them that I am a lifelong learner, and that I am always
trying to excel and succeed. Additionally, the students can
see other students' polished works and get ideas for their
writing…
```

school year starts (see Figure 5.1). In documenting work as a professional educator and when interacting with students' families, candidates can go back five years for some of their accomplishments. I heard this stuff from the beginning, but I didn't really understand what it meant or how to begin until I read the directions and saw a few excerpts. Once I read and reread the entry directions, I began to break down my accomplishments to mirror the areas that were mandatory to cover as well as the areas I could optionally cover. There was a useful organizational chart in my materials that I filled in as I began my planning. See Figure 5.2 for my variation of this chart.

I didn't know how many accomplishments I should include. Two? Ten? Fifty? I searched, studied, and read everything to find advice on this.

Figure 5.2

Organizational Chart				
Category	Activity	Significance	Impact	Documentation
Mandatory: Interactive communication with families [current year]				
Effort to understand parents' concerns [current year]				
Contributions connecting school to community [last five years]				

(NBPTS, AYAELA Entry 6, 11)

"It's up to you" is all I heard. I also wanted to know the most desirable way to document accomplishments. Did they prefer letters or signatures or what? But again, no one had an answer to my question, so I had to decide for myself. I found useful references in the "Assembling Your Entry" section; there were two ways candidates could prepare their responses. One was the continuous essay approach, and the other was the discrete sets approach. Both used an example that said, "You may have chosen to include six descriptions . . ." I jumped on this number, "Ah haaaa!" and decided I would have six accomplishments. Hey, it was the only specific number I could find anywhere! Because there were three main categories listed in the chart to document for each entry, I decided I would have two accomplishments in each category. As I said, I am a systematic person. Creating structure like this helped me feel in control and, therefore, improved my confidence.

Next I had to go through all my accomplishment options to decide on the best two accomplishments for each category. Examples for documenta-

Figure 5.3

```
┌─────────────────────────────────────────────────────────────────┐
│                                                                   │
│   Verification form                                               │
│                                                                   │
│   Is the candidate's description of his or her activities accurate?│
│                                                                   │
│   ____✓__ Yes          _____ No        _____ Don't know     │
│                                                                   │
│   How do you know of these activities?                            │
│                                                                   │
│        I have been the state coordinator for the NCTE program to  │
│   recognize excellence in student literary magazines since 1996.  │
│   Each year I have asked Mandy to serve as a judge, and she has   │
│   willingly agreed. She has been a fair, competent judge.         │
│                                                                   │
│   Signature _____                               │
│   Name _____ Date _____                 │
│   Title _____ Phone number _____                │
│   Address _____                 │
│                                                                   │
└─────────────────────────────────────────────────────────────────┘
```

tion options had included artifacts (e.g., letters sent and received and logs), as well as verification forms from various people. Since no one could tell me exactly how many verification forms I should use and how many artifacts, I just tried to use a variety. Whenever I found a strong artifact, I used it because they were so much harder to come by than the simple verification forms (see Figure 5.3). Also, I was allowed fifteen pages of documentation for my six accomplishments, so I made sure I had at least two documents for each. I tried to use a lot of different people to verify my accomplishments: students, parents, colleagues, community members, and so on. I felt good about these decisions, for I had created reasons to back them up, and felt my entries were strong as a result.

Moving Through the Assessment Process

By the time we had our second university meeting, I was working on my accomplishment entries and gathering materials for my classroom entries. Up to this point, I had felt uncomfortable with the idea of videotaping because, with all the microphone-type descriptions and warnings, it seemed too complicated. I was glad we had set aside some time to talk about details of videotaping in our university class.

Unfortunately our meeting initially made me more anxious! We spent the majority of our time discussing microphone types and functions, how important it was to hear your students on the video, and details like "do a forty-five degree turn of camera every thirty seconds." My only practice at that point had been to set up a camera in the corner of my room and tape myself teaching. It showed only me and the backs of a few students' heads; their voices could not be heard on the tape!! At our meeting I realized I was going to need help to accomplish the video part of the process, so my attention and my worries turned to who could help me.

The most beneficial part of our meeting was viewing a sample National Board lesson on video; it really helped my anxiety level because it wasn't perfect. It showed the cameraman moving and the movement was a bit jerky. The teacher was interacting with the students, but at times several of them were talking at once and could not be heard. In other words, it was realistic, and that was a relief.

Some of our school district technology people offered to come video-tape us, which was another relief—to have someone offer to help! Most people ended up using their own students to videotape them, which seemed to work out fine. I was very lucky in that at my school we had the magnet program for video broadcasting, so we had numerous students being trained to videotape (among other things). I was luckier than most of my colleagues because I had two sources of people to help with my videotaping. I began to feel more confident that I would find a way to get it done.

Do your videos early, in December if you can. The instructions say, "Practice all the time, keep the camera running, have lots of lessons on tape so that you can choose the best one to use and write about." This is all very good advice; however, logistics are a huge, stressful issue with video-taping. They were for me and for almost everyone I talked to. The only absolute that works here is: "There *will* be problems with videotaping, so don't expect to get it right the first time out." I heard horror stories of teachers waiting until the last day and the audio did not come out on the tape, of teachers having to reteach the same lesson because the video didn't turn out right the first time, and of teachers settling for less than ideal videos because they ran out of time. Give yourself options for each lesson. Have two or three quality videotaped lessons as options for each video entry, and do it early. This will radically reduce your anxiety level.

I made one huge mistake when it came to videotaping. Well, actually there were several, but one almost ruined the rest of my school year. Let me explain. I wanted to videotape a class discussion at the end of our study of a novel. The challenge was to schedule the videographer enough ahead of time to secure the date, then make my unit of study dovetail to meet that date. While I knew where I was going in my curriculum, knowing the exact date for a particular lesson three weeks ahead of time is, as any teacher will verify from experience, almost impossible. Nevertheless, I set up my date with the school district's professional videographers to tape two class periods. Then I strictly structured my lessons, kept a fire extinguisher handy, and watched the clouds, praying we wouldn't have a "snow day," thereby missing school and ruining my schedule!

I actually finished the unit a day ahead of schedule but managed to find some filler assignments to delay the final discussion for when the videotaping was scheduled. Then, the inevitable (if you believe in Murphy's law) happened: When I checked in with the district people, I was told they couldn't videotape either class period the following day as planned, "but we can be in there next week for sure." Panic! What was I going to do?

I couldn't postpone the class discussion another day. I didn't have another perfect topic coming up soon enough in either of my courses that would sustain a continuous twenty-minute class discussion. I definitely should have just had one of my own students tape instead of participate in the discussion, but I wanted an expert filmmaker. A light went on. I went to the video broadcast instructor and asked if she could possibly (Please! Please!) loan me a student the following day. It was better than nothing, and I had one shot to get it right.

Here's where the mistake came in. I had told both of my classes we would be videotaped the following day. I had figured my first class would be a good warm-up session for me, and by the time the second class of the day came around, we'd all be more awake and ready, plus they tended to participate more on a daily basis anyway. With this in mind and because my team-teaching schedule allowed me this luxury, I switched the classes so that the more talkative, involved, second class would be the one I'd have when the student filmmaker showed up first thing in the morning. Since I had never made such a switch before, the students knew immediately something was up. Boy were they mad at me by the time they came to the second class! In my panicked, quick thinking, I had totally disregarded my first class and their possible contributions. Not only did they not want to discuss the book as planned, they didn't want to listen to anything I had to say. I had a sense of their anger from my teaching partner and the other students before the first class ended. So by the time they arrived I had arranged for another student to come in and videotape them as well; however, it took a significant amount of class time to explain and apologize repeatedly to get them focused on the task at hand. It was horrible and carried over with a couple of the students for several weeks. My recommendation: Don't forget your students! This process of trying to look brilliant on tape and have the right camera, microphones, and videographer made me lose sight of what it was all about—my students and what I was teaching them!

I had a difficult time deciding which tape to use for my entry; I felt I owed it to my first class (the second group filmed) for slighting them so thoughtlessly, but the tension in the room was obvious on the video. I had to go with my second class (who was filmed first) because their discussion was outstanding. Although the video I submitted is great, I still feel ill at ease when I think about this day and my mistake.

Writing the Entries

When it came time to write the actual entries, I heard stories of my colleagues struggling over what to write, how to fill ten pages, and how to cut down twenty-five-page drafts to ten pages, but this aspect of the process was not hard for me. I enjoy writing and simply needed sustained quiet time so I could focus. I spent nearly every Saturday in January and February writing, revising, and editing. I generally worked more than ten hours a day, sitting in front of my computer on these work days.

I took a few days off from work to complete all my writing (three days were allocated by the school district). What helped me most of all was sharing my drafts with other members of my group at the university. Having them read my stuff and ask me for clarifications helped me make wise revisions and feel confident about my final drafts.

When I began this certification process, I set April 1 as my deadline to mail my portfolio. As I moved toward this date, I kept debating with myself. April 1 was a Saturday, so I might as well use the weekend to finish everything and send it out on Monday, April 3. But my wedding was looming large in the not-too-distant future. Once the invitations were out, I knew I had to finish my portfolio and mail it as soon as possible so that is exactly what I did. I mailed The Box on March 27, and it was received by the NBPTS on Monday, April 3. What a relief!

The Assessment Center

Because the wedding and honeymoon were planned for our spring break in late April, I vowed not to even look at my assessment center materials until school got out. Knowing what I know now, I would not make that vow.

Don't wait too long to start looking over the assessment center stimulus materials that you will receive before your portfolio is due. First, send your portfolio and take a break. Then at least check out the materials you receive to give yourself the option of more preparation time. I wish I had looked at mine earlier than I did. I waited until the end of May to really crack the materials open and read the full contents. And guess what? That gave me less than a month (with finals and year-end responsibilities) to "examine and be familiar with" thirty-four pieces of literature including six novels, four of which I had never read.

In retrospect, I wish I had looked at the list earlier; I could have been reading some of the texts at night. I also received a large packet of stimulus materials that I tackled after school concluded. Everyone's assessment center materials are different. Some areas receive a single page: "Know everything there is to know about science." Some materials are hundreds of pages in a packet, and some, like mine, are a list of things to find on your own as well as articles in a packet. Be informed before you procrastinate.

I ended up doing one heck of a cram session after school got out. I scheduled my testing for the Tuesday after school ended; my husband and I were going on a camping trip the following week. I didn't want to devote my whole summer to studying or worrying about the test. I really needed the time off, so, for the three days I had, I focused, crammed, read, wrote summaries, and talked with colleagues. I did the absolute best I could, given the minimal time I had. Then I went in and took my test. To tell you the truth, it wasn't bad. I felt rather confident throughout my testing. Since the tests were broken into four activities, I took a little break after each one and went out to my car and had some ice water I had stored there in a cooler. Halfway through I had a nice lunch and cleared my head.

Having spent, by this time, more than eight months thinking about my methods, students, assignments, and philosophy, I basically wrote what I knew, and it felt pretty darn good! I can't even begin to describe for you the relief I felt when I walked out of that testing center at the end of the day. I was finally *free*! I had done it and felt good about it and was so very ready to be on my own schedule: camping, hiking, thinking about things other than teaching and students and how to express my understanding of literature and its relevance. Wow! What a wonderful time the summer was for me! Never had I felt I earned a summer off more than I did this one.

Final Thoughts

A few hints for you: Don't even think about the assessment center until your portfolio is finished and has been mailed. It's one more gigantic hurdle to overcome, but once you rest and gain some perspective, it's rather simple to tackle compared to the portfolio entries themselves. To ace the assessment center activities, I suggest you review your materials and remind yourself that you already know what you are doing as a teacher or you wouldn't be pursuing National Board Certification in the first place. Then take a deep breath, don't panic, and go in there and show them what you know. It's kind of fun, really. How often does a teacher get to showcase his or her thoughts and experiences as a teacher? Not often enough! So this is a great opportunity.

Now, as I await my scores, my expectations vacillate. On the one hand, I know I worked extremely hard and feel confident that I passed. I know that, pass or fail, I've learned a great deal about both myself and my profession. I feel like I am a better teacher for having gone through the National Board Certification process. It required me to think about why I do what I do as a teacher, what some more effective approaches are, and where my weaknesses are, and it reminded me to never lose sight of my real focus—my students and their needs.

If I do have to redo a portfolio entry or retake a test at the assessment center, I am going to do it without hesitation, for I know the rigorous process is worthwhile. One day soon I will be able to proudly say, "I am a National Board Certified Teacher!"

Results

I was incredibly anxious awaiting my scores in late November. I logged on to the National Board's web site daily until I finally found a list of newly certified teachers. I was utterly stunned when my name did not appear. I sat staring at the screen, counting the list, rereading, refreshing the screen, and yet my name was not listed. I felt like I had been kicked in the stomach; it was a physically painful experience. I couldn't believe that I hadn't passed. I denied it for days, convincing myself that not all the portfolios had been graded. Several days later when I received my scores in the mail, I could deny it no longer. I had not accumulated enough points to earn a passing score. Stunned is the only way to describe my reaction. I felt embarrassed even; it was a crushing blow because I had worked so long and so hard.

I now know why I did not pass. One of the mistakes I made was not focusing enough on the scoring guide. I read it when I received it, but focused only on my goal—the Level 4 response descriptions. I did not reread or study this guide as I worked on each entry, and I should have. I was so anxious to get finished and focus on my wedding that I just relied on my past successes to carry me through. Hard work had always paid off in the past. I had, indeed, worked hard on every entry, but I had not worked smart. Allowing myself more time to prepare for the assessment center tests and studying the scoring guide to ensure I met every criterion for each entry were essential steps I did not take.

When the shock and embarrassment died down, I sat down and pored through the two entries I had decided to redo. It was obvious why I had scored so low; I simply did not meet the requirements for a Level 4 score. I am now, once again, working on my National Board Certification. I chose to redo my two low classroom-based entries because they were weighted the heaviest in the scoring division (15 percent each). Improvements on these two entries could increase my overall score the most.

Going through the National Board Certification process has been a worthwhile experience. Analyzing my methods, practices, rationale, and assessment procedures have been invaluable. The process helped me choose better assignments and identify valid reasons for my teaching methods and content.

Not passing the first time around was a humbling experience. I felt like a failure initially. Many of my colleagues passed and, while I was genuinely thrilled for them, I was gravely disappointed in myself. Ultimately, the process made me realize that I can and need to push myself to do more, to try new things, and to continue striving for my best if I want to be an excellent teacher. The National Board Certification process has reminded me that excellence in teaching is a lifelong process, and teachers have room to grow if they are willing to push themselves. So although I have not achieved my goal yet, perseverance prevails. I am still committed to being one of the first teachers in my state to achieve this certification.

All Those Questions

Diane Barone

Any teacher who wonders about seeking certification by the National Board for Professional Teaching Standards (NBPTS) will have questions about it. Lots of questions. Possibly, you are a teacher who has investigated the process thoroughly and feel comfortable about the expectations. Perhaps most of your questions relating to the process have been answered. Or maybe you are a teacher who has heard bits and pieces about this process and you want to learn more before you commit your time and money to it. In this chapter, I try to respond to your potential questions. However, if I have missed your burning question, you can always visit the National Board's web site (www.nbpts.org). If the answer is not on the web site, you can write or call the NBPTS office (1-800-22TEACH); someone always answers.

Before I begin posing and answering questions, I do want to remind you of rumors. There are innumerable rumors about this process. Whatever the rumor might be, it always results in additional stress for candidates. Some of the rumors may come from the chat rooms for teachers, and others may come from other teachers working with you on this process. Most chat rooms are not monitored so there can be all kinds of inaccuracies written on them along with useful information. If you are in doubt about the veracity of a rumor, check with your local facilitator, go to the National Board's web site, call the National Board offices, or visit one of the five resource centers on-line. The resource centers are located at Bank Street College (www.bankstreet.edu/html/nbpts), Florida A&M University (norish.adams@famu.edu), Illinois State University (www.coe.ilstu.edu/ilnbpts), University of Texas at El Paso (hvizdak@utep.edu), and Stanford University (http://nbrc.stanford.edu). The centers work with schools and university faculty on standards-based teacher development. It is essential that during this process you have accurate information, and these resources should help with that.

Additionally, it is very important to remember that the National Board consistently revises and improves the certificate expectations. For example, this year most of the certificates have been revised and the NBPTS now offers Next Generation certificates. Certificate areas that were new last year did not undergo revision. So if you are a candidate in Adolescent and Young Adult Physical Education this year, you would get accurate information from a candidate who engaged in the process last year. It will be the same for both of you. However, if you are a candidate as an Early Childhood Generalist, your certificate expectations are different from those who sought this certificate last year. In fact, you will have to meet additional standards. It is not necessary for you to know the previous expectations or to compare them to the new ones. You just need to be sure that you are paying close attention to the specific requirements and standards of your newly revised certificate.

With this in mind, it is time to move to questions that you might need answered before deciding to engage in this process or while you are a part of it. I have divided them into big questions and picky questions; then I discuss what a cohort group might provide.

Big Questions

Why would a teacher choose to engage in the National Board Certification process?

This is *the* big question, which you will need to think through before you engage in this process. When I have asked teachers why they made this decision, I have received a variety of answers. This is not surprising because the teachers who engage in this process vary from relatively new teachers to teachers who have multiple years of experience, among other differences. As you read through the reasons, you may recognize your reason for entering this process or you may want to add to the list. Following are some of the reasons that have been given:

- I wanted to demonstrate that I could teach to the highest standards. I wanted to demonstrate to myself that I could do this.

- I wanted to demonstrate that I could teach to the highest standards. I wanted all the parents of the children I teach to know this. I wanted the community to know this.

- I wanted the folks out there who are bashing teachers to know that there are accomplished teachers in their community. I wanted this board certification because most of these people understand the board certification that physicians get.

- I wanted to stay in the classroom and I wanted a way to be recognized for the work that I do.

- I finished my master's and I wanted to engage in more professional development.

- I wanted to become a leader in my district and state and now I can provide professional development for other teachers.

- I wanted a pay increase. And in my district I get an increase for all the years that I am certified.

How do I know when the time is right for me to engage in this process?

From the stories shared in this book, you have most likely realized that there is no perfect time. However, you will be ready for this process after you have studied the standards in your area and have been able to document explicitly that you teach to them. For example, if you rarely allow your students to engage in conversation about their learning, you may want to work on this as you get ready for this process. Or if you have infrequently participated in professional communities where you have provided leadership to other teachers, you may want to move outside your classroom and develop these experiences before beginning the process. On the other hand, if these experiences and others are routine to you, then you are ready to begin.

After your expertise as a teacher, time is the factor to consider. This is big. Most teachers who choose to be involved with this process are busy inside and outside of their classrooms. They work with their students before and after school. They frequently meet with parents. And they take on curricular or other responsibilities in their schools, districts, states, and so on. In the midst of such a busy professional life, a teacher must find 200 to 400 hours for this process. This is no small endeavor. Try it yourself. Take a calendar and see if you can block out this much time from June or July until April. Remember, most of the work for this process occurs during your academic year.

Finally, I have adapted and revised a questionnaire from the support network of the National Board. I ask each teacher who is considering this process to complete the quiz. This is basically how it goes. For each question you can score yourself with a 1 (strong no) to a 7 (strong yes). Then add all your scores. If your score is from 75 to 63, then you are ready. If it is from 62 to 50, you can do it but it may be difficult. And if your score is from 49 to 37, you need to wait a while and work on changing some areas so that you are better prepared. Following are the questions:

1. I have 200 to 400 hours to work on this process.

2. I am a self-starter and organized in the way that I work.

3. I can teach to high standards.

4. I enjoy working with other professionals.

5. I routinely analyze students' work and then use this information to guide my teaching.

6. I feel comfortable sharing videos of my teaching practice.

7. I feel comfortable writing about my teaching and sharing this with others for constructive feedback.

8. I often reflect on my teaching and on my students' learning and then modify instruction based on what I discover.

9. I have no problem meeting with a cohort group on Saturdays.

10. I can find someone who will be willing to read my work and offer constructive feedback. Not just "good" or "wow."

11. My family and colleagues are ready to support me.

12. I have a computer or access to one on a routine basis.

13. I have no major life events happening this year (e.g., a new baby, marriage, and divorce).

14. I am healthy.

15. I can afford $2,300.00 for this process.

Okay, the time is right. How do I apply?

The application process is straightforward. Just remember: To engage in this process, you have to have graduated from an accredited college or university, have a current teaching credential, and have completed at least three years of teaching. If you meet these criteria, the steps to follow are:

1. Call the National Board at 1-800-22TEACH or go to the web site (www.nbpts.org) and request an application. It usually takes about four weeks to receive a mailed application. The best time to apply is in the summer or early fall. Your completed application must be returned to the National Board by December 1, along with a check for $300.00.

2. Decide which certificate area is best for you. The application book will help you make this decision. For each certificate area, it has questions to guide you in this process. For example, the following questions help a teacher decide if he or she wants to be a Middle Childhood Generalist.

   For the portfolio, will you be able to

   - demonstrate that your teaching practice meets the middle childhood generalist standards?
   - have access to a class of at least six students, with at least 51 percent of the students in the class ages 7 through 12 as of December 31, 2002?
   - submit student work samples and videotapes in English and/or Spanish showing your interactions with your students?
   - explain how you use a topic in writing to develop students' thinking and writing skills for different audiences through the use of narrative and expository student work samples?

- discuss how you help students better understand a big idea in science using relevant science and mathematics knowledge, and engage students in work that helps to enrich their understanding of the interdisciplinary areas?
- show how you create a climate that supports students' emerging abilities to understand and consider perspectives other than their own and to assume responsibility for their own actions through a social studies topic?
- present evidence of how you impact student learning through your work outside of the classroom as you interact with students' families, your colleagues, and other professionals?

For the assessment center, will you be able to demonstrate content knowledge and pedagogical content knowledge in areas such as

- English language arts?
- mathematics?
- science?
- social studies?
- the arts?
- health?

(National Board for Professional Teaching Standards 2001, p. 15)

3. Send your completed application and $300.00 to the National Board.

4. The National Board will send you your box, which you will receive in about three weeks. Sometimes certain certificate areas are delivered at different times. These times are always noted in the application materials.

5. The National Board expects you to complete certain forms and return them quickly. These forms document that you have taught for three years, are currently employed, and have graduated from an accredited institution. These forms usually are mailed to you, not enclosed in The Box.

6. Open your box and get familiar with the materials in it. Find the forms first and look at what needs to be done. For example, one form needs to be sent to each parent or legal guardian to document permission to videotape their children and use their work samples for your portfolio. Only children for whom their parents have given permission may be included in your entries. Start working on the Professional Involvement and Parent Communication entry immediately.

7. Send the remainder of your fee ($2,000.00) to the National Board by the deadline, usually in January.

All that is left to do now is complete your portfolio entries and the assessment center responses.

What is a passing score?

The passing score is 275. However, you do not need to pass each entry to be successful. Each entry receives a score and each is weighted. Typically, the portfolio entries centered on your teaching and student learning are weighted most. The Family Communication and Professional Community entry then follows these in weighting. The assessment center activities have the lowest weights attached to them.

How is my work evaluated and how do I learn about what I have done?

All completed entries are sent to one location. At this location, all entries are sorted by certificate area. Don't panic that your entry will be lost; each entry has your identification number on it because you put it there. The sorting works something like this. All similar certificate areas are sorted by entry. Then, entries are sent to regional scoring centers. For example, all Parent Communication and Professional Community entries for Early Childhood Generalist will be sent to one site.

Assessors who have been prepared to score your work are waiting for it. At the site, teachers, some National Board Certified Teachers and others who have expertise in your area, are trained to score entries. They receive two days of training with the rubric that they will use to score your entry. If they are unreliable in scoring during training, they are dismissed.

Teachers are recruited by the National Board to be scorers. Any teacher who is not currently involved in the National Board process can qualify. The National Board provides remuneration for teachers who engage in the scoring. More details about being involved in this process are available on the National Board's web site.

When your work is scored, the assessor is marking down places where you have met the standards. Assessors mark down only positive evidence. This process, as reflected in scoring, is not a deficit process. The scorer is not looking for what you did not do; he or she is only considering what you have done. This information contributes to the final score. Each scorer begins by assigning an entry a 3. Then as he or she reads through your work, views your video, or does both, this score of 3 is raised or lowered based on the evidence that you have provided. Because of the way entries are scored, you will receive only a number score. Some teachers have been upset with this because they wanted more information. Because of the way entries are scored, however—recording only positive instances of standards met—this information is not provided to candidates. The best advice for a candidate who does not receive the score he or she would like in an entry is to review the standards and critically analyze the evidence that was provided to demonstrate teaching to these standards.

After each entry is scored, the scores are reported to the testing company. The company then compiles all your scores to complete the final report that determines whether you have passed.

When do I learn my results?

It traditionally has taken until late November or early December to learn results. The procedure at present is for teachers to be notified on the National Board's web site and by letter. For four days only teachers who have participated in the process will be able to access the site. In this way, each teacher can find out his or her results in private. After these days, the web site is available to the whole world. The names of all successful teachers are posted. The NBPTS does not post the names of teachers who were not successful.

What if I am not successful?

The National Board's policy allows you to bank scores of successful entries, those with scores of 2.75 or higher. A teacher can redo any entry with a lower score than this. The National Board marks the entries that can be retaken by a teacher. Each candidate has two years for retakes. The scores of retakes are then compiled with the banked scores for the results. It is important to know that whether it is higher or lower the new score replaces the old one. As a result, candidates need to think carefully about which entries they might retake. For example, they need to think about the weighting of scores. In one entry a small gain might result in a large point change because of the weighting. Also, if a candidate does extremely poorly in one entry, he or she needs to think about how likely it will be that a significantly higher score can be achieved. This person will need to create a plan to explicitly meet the standards required in this entry and to make sure they include analytical and reflective writing.

The hardest part of the retake process for candidates is that they have to wait until the following year for results. They hear their results at the same time as candidates who are engaging in this process for the first time.

Why does the National Board revise their certificate requirements?

The National Board revises the certificate requirements for several reasons. One relates directly to testing issues. When the first certificates were developed, there was oversampling to make sure that the scorers had enough evidence to validly make decisions about a teacher's performance. As the certificates were scored over several years and as teachers complained about the redundancy of what they had to submit, the National Board decided to revise certificates to reduce the redundancy, but maintain validity. The certificate areas receiving the most revision were the generalist certificates because they were the oldest ones. However, all the certificates, the Next Generation certificates, are similar in the number of entries and assessment center activities.

National Board members continually meet to discuss the standards. In the Next Generation entries, each teacher now has additional standards to meet. Although there is variability among the standards required for entries, teachers now have to meet standards based on equity and technology.

The National Board also determined that the assessment center activities needed to be changed. Of the numerous changes, the most dramatic is that the assessment center activity now takes one half-day rather than a whole day. Teachers are responding to prompts that are very different from those in the past. Previously, teachers responded to prompts requiring lengthy responses. Now the prompts are more focused on content and require thirty-minute responses. The procedures have changed as well. Teachers can no longer bring materials into the test center. This change in procedure complements the change in the types of responses expected of teachers. And the National Board keeps working with the testing folks so that the computer screens display the questions in a more candidate-friendly manner. Teachers now see questions and data in a split-screen format so that they no longer have to scroll to review material necessary to consider for their responses.

Because the National Board is always looking to improve the assessments, there will always be change in expectations or procedures. The changes are put in place to improve the assessments and the process. And the National Board is very careful when these changes are made that candidates suffer no negative consequences. For example, whenever there are major changes in a certificate, each entry is scored by two assessors, rather than one. Their scores are compared; if there is a significant difference between the scores, a third assessor is called in to score.

Now that I am engaged in this process, I would like to see completed entries from National Board teachers so that I have a better idea of what is expected. Is this possible?

Completed portfolios are not available to candidates to view. They are held by the National Board teachers and candidates and are not in circulation because that could compromise the National Board process. However, National Board teachers and candidates are often willing to sit with new candidates and walk them through their materials. They enjoy sharing the decisions they made and what they would do differently if they were to engage in the process again. To find National Board teachers in your area, visit the National Board's web site, where you will see a list of National Board Certified Teachers by state. You might then contact one or more of these teachers to talk with you about the process.

Picky Questions

If I become certified, how long does this certification last?

Your certification will last ten years.

Is there a way that I can recertify after the ten years have expired so that I can continue to be National Board Certified?

The National Board is working on a recertification process right now. It should be in place by 2005. The current thinking is that teachers will not have to do the whole process again, but will undertake a variation of the process for renewal. Details about this process are still being developed.

I want to engage in this process, but I am a specialist in my building and I don't have my own classroom. Can I do this?

Yes, you can. You will need to borrow a class, though. The ideal is to borrow a class whose teacher's philosophy and style are similar to yours. In this way, the children will benefit from having two teachers. Otherwise, if you are very different from the classroom teacher, the children will have to constantly adjust and they may find this difficult to do.

I am working with a team teacher. We both want to engage in this process. Will this be a problem?

It will not be a problem. At the beginning of each entry, you will be asked to talk about your class, providing a description of your teaching situation. This is the place to make it explicit that you are part of a team and describe how you and your partner have created your classroom learning community. It will be important for you to stand out as an individual as well. Your voice must come through in your entries, especially as you talk about how you meet the learning needs of your students alone and with your partner.

I am confused about my years of teaching experience. Do they all have to be in one school?

No. You just need to demonstrate that you have been teaching for at least three years. Your school secretary should be able to document your years of experience; you should not have to go to your previous schools to get this documentation. Your school district's personnel director also has this information.

Should I tell my principal that I am involved in this process?

Yes! Your principal needs to be a part of this process. Some school principals consider work on National Board Certification as part of your annual evaluation. Beyond evaluation, your principal needs to know that National Board Certification results in

1. improved teacher quality as a result of looking carefully at your practice and your students.

2. recognition of accomplished teachers and their commitment to improve their teaching.

3. expanded leadership capacity as National Board teachers become more involved in leadership activities tied to student learning.

4. enhanced professional culture of his or her school.

In addition, your principal can support you in this process. He or she could help by finding equipment or a person to do the videotaping for you. He or she could read your work and provide constructive feedback or editing. And, perhaps most important, your principal could relieve you of some duties so that you can focus solely on the assessment process for one year.

Should I involve the parents of my students in this process?
Yes! As with your principal and for some of the same reasons, parents need to be involved. Parents can also provide documentation of the work that you do with their children.

Can I use my master's degree in the professional community entry?
Yes. However, it is not sufficient to say that you received a master's and that shows how you are a lifelong learner. You need to show how your working on this degree changed your teaching and how it has resulted in students' learning.

I am working on the Professional Community and Family Involvement entry. Should I put a lot of things in this entry or should I focus on only a few activities?
There is no easy answer here. You need to select evidence that provides a clear, consistent, and compelling picture of your involvement with families and your professional community. Just listing activities will not demonstrate this. There is no magic number of entries.

In compiling your evidence for this entry, consider the strongest evidence that ties to student learning in your classroom or in the classrooms of other teachers. And as with all entries, think about organization. Many teachers have grouped their professional community evidence by their classroom, school, district, state, and so on.

I have a great video. It is twenty-two minutes long. Will the National Board assessor evaluate it all?
No! Each entry has certain restrictions. For videos, there is a time length restriction. For commentaries, there are page length and font restrictions. The National Board has created these restrictions so that the process is equitable for all candidates. If you send a twenty-two-minute video and the expectation was for twenty minutes, then the assessor will look only at the first twenty minutes of the video. If the best part of the video is at the end, it is unfortunate because no one will see it but you.

I have twenty pages allotted for my commentary, but I wrote only eighteen pages. Will that be a problem?

There is no clear answer here. You can write entries that are shorter than the maximum page length. The shorter page length will not be scored against you. It is more important to consider how well you answered the necessary questions. Did you include descriptive, analytical, and critical writing about your teaching and your students' learning? Did you address all the necessary standards? Did you present clear, consistent, and convincing evidence? If you answered yes to all these questions, then you are fine. If the answer was no, then you might want to use some of that space until you can answer these questions in the affirmative.

When I read through an entry, I noticed all these details about font, margins, and page length. Do I really have to follow these directions?

Yes! These specifications guarantee equity. The rules are the same for all candidates. The font issue also relates to the scorers. In the past, 10-point type was acceptable. However, after listening to the scorers discuss the fatigue that developed from reading these small-font entries, all entries now have to be written in 12-point type. Don't stress though, the National Board has adjusted the length requirements to accommodate the larger 12-point type.

Cohort Support Through the Process

You may be wondering how to get the best support as you work through this process. Certainly, you want support from family and school. In many communities, cohort groups have been formed to support teachers as well. Generally, these groups meet periodically throughout the entire process. The support they offer differs as candidates move through the process. Following is an overview of the support that might be provided:

- The cohort facilitator provides information about the process and how to apply. He or she is available to teachers to answer questions about the process.

- Once teachers have decided to participate, the facilitator brings the group of teachers together for support meetings.

- *Meeting 1.* Teachers talk about the core propositions and how they teach to these. They review the standards in their certificate areas. Teachers look through their materials and work through the "Getting Started" section in their boxes. They learn about the organization of entries, writing expectations, vocabulary, videotaping, and so on. Teachers build a schedule for completing this process. Teachers might listen to a panel of National Board teachers talk about the process.

- *Meeting 2.* Teachers work together on the Parent Communication and Professional Accomplishment entry. They brainstorm all the ways that they do this and talk about the way their students' learning has been influenced.

- *Meeting 3 and subsequent meetings.* Teachers meet and constructively provide feedback to each other about their commentaries and video-tapes. Teachers are expected to come with a commentary, video, or both for this work. They also bring a form to record the constructive feedback that they receive. This form is divided in half with a section for the commentary and one for the video. The top of the form lists the standards the teacher has to address. In the example, just numbers appear; however, the teacher would write in the specific standards that they had to document such as engagement, equity, or content. Following is an example of this form:

	Standard 1	2	3	4	5	6
Commentary						
Video						

As members of the cohort work with a teacher's entry or video, in the appropriate box they record all the instances of the teacher demonstrating a standard (Note: The boxes are bigger in the form brought by the teacher so the teacher has space to write.). These responses show the teacher clearly where he or she has met the standards and where this has not happened. This constructive feedback provides every teacher with the necessary information to improve his or her entries.

- *Meeting in January.* Teachers talk about the assessment center. They work together in similar certificate areas to prepare for this experience.

Beyond the meetings, the cohort members have celebrations. Often the teachers celebrate when they have sent their boxes to the NBPTS. In some places, all the teachers go to the post office together to send their boxes on their way. There is typically a celebration at the end of the process when all the teachers have completed their portfolios and assessment center activities. These celebrations always precede the posting of final scores.

Now that you have answers to many questions, some of which you may not have even considered, it is time to get busy. Put this book away for a while and get started. Make a schedule to complete the process. Talk to your students, parents, colleagues, and principal about what you are doing. Start an entry. If you have questions as you go, return to this book, talk to your facilitator, or go to a web site for information. Appendix B lists web sites that you might visit for support.

Congratulations on your decision to enter into this professional development activity. Upon your successful completion, you will enter a special group of teachers known to others as accomplished teachers, teachers who make a difference to students' learning!

Portfolio Samples

Carol Hines

My portfolio entry on social issues covered a mini-unit on slavery and the Orphan Train. It's a powerful unit providing students with the opportunity to learn, compare, analyze, and reflect on two different yet similar events in our history, relate them to the Civil Rights Movement, and to minority issues today. The information learned impacts them emotionally leading to thoughtful and insightful discussions and writing. The rubric used during the videotaped group discussion and the student discussion sheet, used for personal reflection, are provided as well as the student's poem about the Orphan Train.

SLAVERY/ORPHAN TRAIN/CIVIL RIGHTS DISCUSSION

Name _Natalie_ _____ Period _5°_   _200_

1. Using the information you learned researching your famous African American in History, how do you think their life would have been different if they had been alive today and not when they were? List specific examples.

   they could do what they want + have more opportunities

2. Since the Civil Rights Movement in the 1960s, how have the following changed? List specific examples.
   a. Discrimination:

   everyone must be created equal
   b. Educational opportunities:

   everyone has the right to get a good education
   c. Employment opportunities:

   children aren't allowed to work + race should't make a differents

3. Have you or anyone you know been discriminated against? What happened and how did you or they feel about it? Be specific.

   Yes. some of my friends wanted to play in the boys 3on3   getting a
   tournement. They asked + the people in charge said there would be   job

4. List current examples of discrimination in our community.   one for girls. The were madt
   kids in other schools talking bad about   first but then they under-
   other kids in schools.   stead.

5. How can we stop this from happening again?

   talk to people, set good examples + be kind to everyone

6. How have children's opportunities, protections, and legal rights changed since the Orphan Train? Be specific.

   kids can't work befor a certain age + no one can enslave other people

7. Are there people in slavery today? If not, why? If yes, give examples of who and where.

   Yes. in other countries people are taking women + children.

8. How did Slavery, the Orphan Train, and the Civil Rights Movements benefit people in the future? Be specific.

   new laws stopped that

9. What can we do to make sure these situations don't reoccur? Be specific.

   confince people it is wrong

10. Out of everything you have learned about these issues, which events, people, or actions will you remember for a long time.

    how people treated slaves + how misrable the slaves must have been on the slave ships.

PREDICT HOW YOU SEE THESE ITEMS CHANGING IN YOUR LIFETIME:

ENSLAVEMENT	CHILD LABOR/CUSTODY LAWS	DISCRIMINATION
1.	1. in Seattle the World Trade Org. are being protested by people	1.
2.	2. companies around the world will stop child labor	2.
3.	3.	3.

If you could talk with a former slave what questions would you ask and WHY?

1. Did you ever really think of running away? because it must have been a horrible life.

2. Where did you live before you were captured?

If you could talk with a former slave owner what questions would you ask and WHY?

1. Why did you enslave people?

2. Did you ever regret what horrible things you did to people?

If you could talk with a child from the Orphan Train what questions would you ask and WHY?

1. What kind of work did you have to do?

2. How old were you & where were you when you were taken away?

If you could talk with an Orphan Train official what questions would you ask and WHY?

1. Did you ever feel sorry for what you did?

2. Did you ever think how badly you were hurting these young children?

If you could talk with a 1960s Civil Rights Activist what questions would you ask and WHY?

1. What hardships did you go through?

2. What made you decide to do what you did?

If you could talk with a 1960s Segregationist what questions would you ask and WHY?

same 1. What hardships did you go through?

2. What made you decide to do what you did?

How have these previous events effected your position, rights and privileges?

1. child labor laws protect me

2. in our country slavery isn't permitted.

How do you see these events continuing to effect your life in the future? Be specific.

1. people are realizing the things they are doing wrong

2. people are becoming more equal everyday

What issues today could be the questions asked in the future?

1. Kosovo situation

2. child labor in different countries

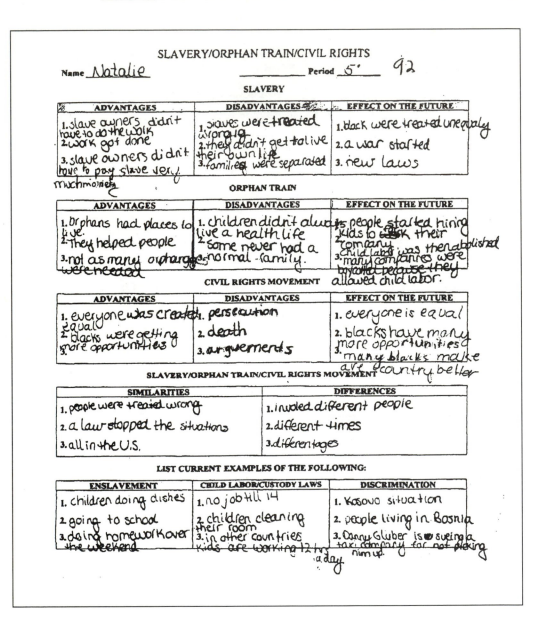

SLAVERY/ORPHAN TRAIN/CIVIL RIGHTS

Name __Natalie__   Period __5°__   92

SLAVERY

ADVANTAGES	DISADVANTAGES	EFFECT ON THE FUTURE
1. slave owners didn't have to do the work 2. work got done 3. slave owners didn't have to pay slave very much money	1. slaves were treated wrong 2. they didn't get to live their own life 3. families were separated	1. black were treated unequaly 2. a war started 3. new laws

ORPHAN TRAIN

ADVANTAGES	DISADVANTAGES	EFFECT ON THE FUTURE
1. orphans had places to live. 2. They helped people 3. not as many orphanges were needed	1. children didn't always live a health life 2. Some never had a normal family.	1. people started hiring kids to work their company 2. child labor was then abolished 3. many companies were boycotted because they allowed child labor.

CIVIL RIGHTS MOVEMENT

ADVANTAGES	DISADVANTAGES	EFFECT ON THE FUTURE
1. everyone was created equal 2. blacks were getting more opportunities	1. persecution 2. death 3. arguements	1. everyone is equal 2. blacks have many more opportunities 3. many blacks make our country better

SLAVERY/ORPHAN TRAIN/CIVIL RIGHTS MOVEMENT

SIMILARITIES	DIFFERENCES
1. people were treated wrong 2. a law stopped the situations 3. all in the U.S.	1. involved different people 2. different times 3. different ages

LIST CURRENT EXAMPLES OF THE FOLLOWING:

ENSLAVEMENT	CHILD LABOR/CUSTODY LAWS	DISCRIMINATION
1. children doing dishes 2. going to school 3. doing homework over the weekend	1. no job till 14 2. children cleaning their room 3. in other countries kids are working 12 hrs a day.	1. Kosovo situation 2. people living in Bosnia 3. Danny Gluber is sueing a taxi company for not picking him up.

THE CHILDREN OF THE ORPHAN TRAIN

The Orphan Train gave children homes,
But led others into slavery.
The happy ones had all the love,
The sad ones only misery.

Children cried as they lost family and friends,
But smiled as they gained a foster family.
Some were not chosen, so they had to move on,
To a place like Mississippi.

Some children cried and some children laughed,
On the train ride to another town.
When they got there, they tried to look their best,
So potential parents would not frown.

After the parents picked the final children,
The rest, disappointed but anxious, boarded the train.
They began their journey to the next stop,
Praying that they wouldn't be disappointed again.

Portfolio Samples

Jeannine Paszek

Student Work Entry

Following are several pages from a student work entry. In
these samples, Jeannine Paszek is showing the student work
and how she responded to it. Accompanying these samples was
her written description of the importance of the student
work, what she learned, and how she will shape instruction
to build on this student's current understandings.

Galena High School

Volume 1, Issue 1

March 2001

COPPER MINING LAB

YOUR LAB WRITE-UP

TITLE

PROBLEM

BACKGROUND

HYPOTHESIS

PROCEDURE

RESULTS

CONCLUSION　　6

Points to remember:

* *Matter cannot be created or destroyed.*

* *Stoichiometry involves the quantitative relationships that exist between the reactants and products.*

* *How is the limiting reactant of a chemical reaction determined?*

* *How is the percent yield of a chemical reaction calculated?*

* *Why might a chemist working in a chemical plant be interested in percent yield?*

* *What are some reasons why actual yield is often lower than expected yield?*

GALENA CHEMISTRY STUDENTS PRODUCE COPPER FROM IRON!

Copper, silver, and gold are often called the coinage metals because at one time they were used primarily to make coins. These metals are often found in the free, elemental state in nature and are also easily obtained from their compounds. As a consequence, they were the first metals known to early humans. Copper has been used since about 5000 BC. By 3000BC, it was discovered that adding tin to copper forms a harder alloy, which is known as bronze. The introduction of this alloy marks the beginning of the Bronze Age. Silver and gold have been known at least as long as copper has—and perhaps even longer. The coinage metals, prized for their resistance to corrosion and for their beauty, are all commercially important. However, they are not particularly abundant elements. In terms of their crustal abundance, copper ranks 25th, silver 64th, and gold 71st among the elements. Do you think their value has anything to do with

The Statue of Liberty in New York harbor is made of copper.

their abundance? Check out the stock exchange! How are these metals obtained? What determines the actual yield? Once they are obtained, what is the process used to extract the pure metal? Are some mining operations more "environmentally friendly" than others? These questions, and more, are some of the problems that must be addressed before any mining operation in the United States can begin. For a mining operation, what's the bottom line? How does mining contribute to our national economy? How about our state economy? Do you know anyone who works in mining?

THE PROBLEM—WHAT IS THE PERCENT YIELD OF COPPER IN THE REACTION BETWEEN COPPER SULFATE AND IRON?

I. Your job is to design a lab that will solve the problem listed above of extracting copper from its compound. Use what you have learned in previous labs about solubility, types of reactions, limiting reactants and percent yield.

II. You must design a method using only the materials provided below:

* Equipment (see attached list)
* 12.5 grams Copper sulfate
* 50 mL Water
* 2.24 grams Iron filings
* Safety equipment / clothing / procedures

Your Name _____

Copper Mining Lab Write-up

Make sure that each of the following points have been addressed in your lab write-up!

Skills	Value	Score
Question		
Question section included as part of lab write-up	1	
Background Information		
Three background resources, one must be from Internet	30	
Background information section demonstrates an understanding of the problem; includes information from prior activities / labs. Balanced equations are written and theoretical products are determined. Mathematical equations that support your theories are clearly shown.	20	
Hypothesis		
Testable-shows understanding of investigation.	5	
Experiment		
Designs an experiment directly related to the hypothesis		
Experiment is clear, and easy to follow		
Contributes to the lab group	10	
Observations and Results		
Records all observations and data accurately; data tables created where possible to record information		
Actual yield calculated; calculations shown	10	
Conclusion		
Original question answered; reflected on hypothesis		
Establish relationship of observations to conclusions		
Provide a reasonable explanation of results		
Apply conclusions to previous lab activities		
Apply to the "real world"	20	
Safety		
Demonstrates good lab techniques		
Leaves a clean work area	4	
TOTAL		

1. Question: What is the percent yield of copper in the reaction between copper sulfate and iron?

II. Background Info:

Natural copper deposits are found in the vicinity of Lake Superior in northern Michigan, and are mined in economically important qualities. Copper also occurs in small quantities in other parts of the world. Chalcocite and covellite, sulfides of copper, are found in Arizona and Nevada and Cornwall, England. Enargite, a sulfarsenate of copper, is found in various areas of the United States. Azurite, a basic carbonate of copper, is found in France and Australia, and malachite, also a basic carbonate, is found in the Ural Mountains. Tetrahedrite, a sulfantimonide of copper and various other metals, and chrusocolla, a copper silicate, are both widely distributed. An oxide of copper, cuprite, can be found in Cuba, and in Peru a basic chloride called atacamite can be found. Copper is the 25th most abundant element in crustal rocks. In mining copper, steam shovels are used to strip off surface rock to yield copper deposits containing other metals such as gold, silver, and nickel.

Milling begins when a crusher reduces copper ore to small pieces. Water is added to form a mixture called slurry. A ball mill grinds the crushed ore in the slurry into fine particles. The particles become concentrated in a flotation cell, where circulating air mixes the slurry with chemicals to form a copper concentrate. This use of chemical reaction is similar to how copper is produced in this lab. The copper concentrate is then put through a dryer and smelted in a flash smelting furnace; this removes impurities in the form of gases and slag (solid waste), producing copper matte. A converter further purifies the molten copper. The copper is further refined in a fire-refining furnace, yielding crude metallic copper, approximately 98 percent pure. Electrolytic refining refines the copper further still, yielding metal exceeds 99.9 percent purity. The final processing consists of melting the copper metal into cakes, billets, rods, and ingots, which are used to manufacture various copper products. The process is shown on the page following.

Excellent resources!

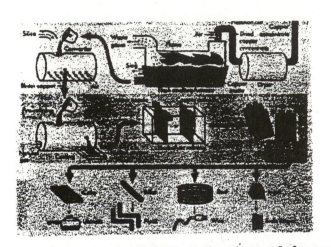

Nice diagram.

Mining can have various detrimental effects on the environment. Surface runoff and subsurface groundwater migrates metals and nonmetals through minesite drainage. The primary minerals are exposed to air/water during mining, and leads to the release, or leaching, of metals and, when sulfide minerals are present, to the generation of acidity. Smelters and mills produce smoke which can have a rather large amount of lead concentration. This smoke can decimate adjacent vegetation in the vicinity. Mining operations involve construction of roads, mining installations, housing for miners, power plants, and dams in often remote, unspoiled locations. This leads to the stripping of large areas of topsoil and flora and fauna in the area.

AS IS THE CASE W/ LEVIATHAN MINE By C.C.

The equation for the reaction between copper sulfate and iron is the following:

$$Cu\,SO_{4\,(aq)} + Fe_{(s)} \longrightarrow Fe_2(SO_4)_{3\,(aq)} + Cu_{(s)}$$

✓Through the Metal Activity Series, we see that iron will replace copper in a single replacement reaction, and that this reaction will in fact take place. Through the Law of Conservation of Mass (which states: "mass can be neither created nor destroyed in an ordinary chemical or physical process"), we know that matter can not be destroyed or created in this reaction, only changed; therefore, we must balance the equation to get equal amounts of each element on each side; the coefficients are 3, 2, 1, and 3, respectively.

Well said!

A limiting reactant is a reactant that there is less of in a reaction, and which inhibits the amount of product produced. To find the limiting reactant you must figure out how much product each reactant produces. The one that produces less is the limiting reactant; the quantity which that reactant produces is the theoretical yield. To find actual yield, what is actually produced through the reaction, one must perform and experiment.

Equations:

$$\frac{12.5 \text{ g CuSO}_4}{} \left| \frac{1 \text{ mol CuSO}_4}{160 \text{ g CuSO}_4} \right| \frac{3 \text{ mol Cu}}{3 \text{ mol CuSO}_4} \left| \frac{64 \text{ g Cu}}{1 \text{ mol Cu}} \right. = 5 \text{ g}$$

$$\frac{2.24 \text{ g Fe}}{} \left| \frac{1 \text{ mol Fe}}{56 \text{ g Fe}} \right| \frac{3 \text{ mol Cu}}{2 \text{ mol Fe}} \left| \frac{64 \text{ g Cu}}{1 \text{ mol Cu}} \right. = 3.84 \text{ g}$$

In this reaction iron is the limiting reactant, and the theoretical yield of copper is 3.84 g.

III. Hypothesis: If a reaction between copper sulfate and iron occurs, then approximately 3 g of copper will be produced as an actual yield with the given amounts of the reactants, giving a percent yield of 78%.

IV. Experiment:

    A. Observe proper safety procedures:
        1. goggles
        2. apron
        3. use beaker tongs when appropriate

    B. Procedure

        1. Measure out 50 mL of water (H2O) in a graduated cylinder. Pour the water into a beaker. Measure an evaporating dish on electronic scale. Record this weight. Re-Zero on dish, and add iron (Fe) into it until weight reaches 2.24 g. Remove dish, Re-Zero scale with nothing on it. Measure out 12.5 g of copper (Cu) on electronic scale, and place in beaker.

        2. Set up Ring stand with a wire gauze on ring. Place beaker on gauze. Light a Bunsen burner beneath the beaker.

        3. Heat solution while stirring with stirring rod.

6. Decant aqueous solution from solid particles while pouring solution from evaporating dish into beaker.

7. Place evaporating dish on ring stand. Heat with Bunsen burner until the copper is fully dried and void of excess liquid.

8. Place evaporating dish on electric scale. Subtract weight of evaporating dish from this weight.

9. Determine percent yield by dividing this value (actual yield) by 3.84 (theoretical yield).

10. Clean up.

V. Results:

Precipitate	Weight E.D. Before	Weight E.D. After	Weight Difference	Color	Odor	Percent Yield
Copper	40.6 grams	45.2 grams	4.6 grams	bronzish tint of brown, pink, red, orange	Odorous, Sulfuric, Smells of burning, as in of	119 % Yield

VI. Conclusion: Our results did not coincide with our hypothesis, nor are they even possible to achieve. Actual yield will at very most be equivalent to theoretical yield, and even then it is very rare. Seeing as actual yield almost always underscores that of theoretical yield, a flaw obviously occurred in the process for a 119 percent yield to occur. This err most likely took place when heating the copper after decanting. The copper might not have been fully dry, the evaporating dish still holding liquid; or, perhaps, the copper oxidized and gained additional weight. While the former culprit is more likely, the latter is also a very possible contribution to the error as well. Upon redoing this experiment, more time and care would be taken into heating the copper product. This chemical extraction of copper is very similar to part of the actual process that takes place in actual copper mining operations. Therefore, it is also clear to see the dangers such operations can cause to the environment. We produced a vast amount of iron sulfate waste in proportion to production of copper. Obviously the wastes produced by copper mines through chemicals and machinery are far greater, and can cause great disaster if precautions aren't taken in such operations.

Make sure that each of the following points have been addressed in your lab write-up!

DUSTIN
00272495

Skills	Points	Score
Question		
Question section included as part of lab write-up	✓	
Background Information		
Three background resources, one must be from Internet	30	30
Background information section demonstrates an understanding of the problem; includes information from prior activities / labs. Balanced equations are written and theoretical products are determined. Mathematical equations that support your theories are clearly shown.	20	20
Hypothesis		
Testable-shows understanding of investigation.	5	5
Experiment		
Designs an experiment directly related to the hypothesis		
Experiment is clear, and easy to follow		
Contributes to the lab group	10	10
Observations and Results		
Records all observations and data accurately; data tables created where possible to record information		
Actual yield calculated; calculations shown	10	10
Conclusion		
Original question answered; reflected on hypothesis		
Establish relationship of observations to conclusions		
Provide a reasonable explanation of results		
Apply conclusions to previous lab activities		
Apply to the "real world"	20	20
Safety		
Demonstrates good lab techniques		
Leaves a clean work area	5	5
TOTAL		

Your group worked well together!

Excellent bibliography!

100 A+
100

Dustin - a very professional job; very proud

Web Site Resources

There are many web sites that can provide support to you as you go through this process. This is just a partial list of those sites. New sites appear on a daily basis. Many of the sites listed here provide links to new sites, so don't worry that you might miss the best ones. Chances are you have already found them.

Primary Web Sites

National Board www.nbpts.org

Bank Street College www.bankstreet.edu/html/nbpts

Florida A&M University norish.adams@famu.edu

Illinois State University www.coe.ilstu.edu/ilnbpts

University of Texas at El Paso hvizdak@utep.edu

Stanford University http://nbrc.stanford.edu

Sites to Explore Standards

The following sites have information about standards in a variety of disciplines. You might refer to them if you want to know the current standards in a content area.

Arts

www.artssedge.kennedy-center.org

Language Arts

International Reading Association www.reading.org

National Council of Teachers of English www.ncte.org

Math

National Council of Teachers of Mathematics www.nctm.org

Health

http://cnn.k12.ar.us

Physical Education

www.aapherd.org

Science

National Science Teachers Association www.NSTA.org

Project 2061 www.project2061.org

GEMS (Great Explorations in Math and Science www.lhs.berkeley.edu

FOSS (Full Option Science System) www.lhs.berkeley.edu

Big Ideas in Science www.scibridge.sdsu.edu

Social Studies

www.socialstudies.org

Candidate Support

Sample Portfolios

www2.ncsu.edu/unity/lockers/project/portfolios/portfolio.html
Two partial portfolio entries and reflections from middle school teachers
of language arts are provided.

General Support

www.wizzlewolf.com/teach.html
This is a super site for information and links to other sites.

www.gse.uci.edu/nbc/nbportfolios.html
This site has resource material.

www.k12.wa.us/cert/nbpts/resources.asp
In addition to general information, this site has information about communicating with parents, principals, and other stakeholders.

Connections to Other Candidates

www.wizzlewolf.com/teach.html

Yahoo e-groups home page www.groups.yahoo.com

References

Bloom, B., M. Engelhart, E. Gurst, W. Hill, and D. Krathwohl. 1984. *Taxonomy of Educational Objectives, Book 1: Cognitive Domains.* Boston: Allyn & Bacon.

Cunningham, J. 1999. "How We Can Achieve Best Practices in Literacy Instruction." In L. Gambrell, L. Morrow, S. Neuman, and M. Pressley, eds., *Best Practices in Literacy Instruction.* pp. 34–48. New York: The Guilford Press.

Day, J. 2001. "How I Became an Exemplary Teacher (Although I'm Really Still Learning Just Like Anyone Else)." In M. Pressley, R. Allington, R. Wharton-McDonald, C. Block, and L. Morrow, eds., *Learning to Read.* pp. 205–218. New York: The Guilford Press.

Dillon, D. 2000. *Reconsidering How to Meet the Literacy Needs of All Students.* Newark, DE: International Reading Association.

Gambrell, L., L. Morrow, S. Neuman, and M. Pressley, eds. 1999. *Best Practices in Literacy Instruction.* New York: The Guilford Press.

National Board for Professional Teaching Standards. (n.d.) *Adolescent and Young Adult English Language Arts Portfolio Materials.* Detroit: National Board for Professional Teaching Standards.

———. (n.d.) *What Teachers Should Know and Be Able to Do.* Detroit: National Board for Professional Teaching Standards.

———. 2001. *2001–2002 Guide to National Board Certification.* Detroit: National Board for Professional Teaching Standards.

Ray, K., and L. Laminack. 2001. "Message from the Editors." *Primary Voices K–6*, 9 (3): 1.